ROBERT
FULTON

Other titles in *Historical American Biographies*

Alexander Graham Bell
Inventor and Teacher
ISBN 0-7660-1096-1

Andrew Carnegie
Steel King and
Friend to Libraries
ISBN 0-7660-1212-3

Annie Oakley
Legendary Sharpshooter
ISBN 0-7660-1012-0

Benjamin Franklin
Founding Father and Inventor
ISBN 0-89490-784-0

Buffalo Bill Cody
Western Legend
ISBN 0-7660-1015-5

Clara Barton
Civil War Nurse
ISBN 0-89490-778-6

Daniel Boone
Frontier Legend
ISBN 0-7660-1256-5

Dolley Madison
Courageous First Lady
ISBN 0-7660-1092-9

Jane Addams
Nobel Prize Winner and Founder
of Hull House
ISBN 0-7660-1094-5

Jeb Stuart
Confederate Cavalry General
ISBN 0-7660-1013-9

Jefferson Davis
President of the Confederacy
ISBN 0-7660-1064-3

Jesse James
Legendary Outlaw
ISBN 0-7660-1055-4

Jim Bowie
Hero of the Alamo
ISBN 0-7660-1253-0

John Wesley Powell
Explorer of the Grand Canyon
ISBN 0-89490-783-2

Lewis and Clark
Explorers of the Northwest
ISBN 0-7660-1016-3

Mark Twain
Legendary Writer and Humorist
ISBN 0-7660-1093-7

Martha Washington
First Lady
ISBN 0-7660-1017-1

Mary Todd Lincoln
Tragic First Lady
of the Civil War
ISBN 0-7660-1252-2

Paul Revere
Rider for the Revolution
ISBN 0-89490-779-4

Robert E. Lee
Southern Hero of the Civil War
ISBN 0-89490-782-4

Robert Fulton
Inventor and
Steamboat Builder
ISBN 0-7660-1141-0

Stonewall Jackson
Confederate General
ISBN 0-89490-781-6

Susan B. Anthony
Voice for Women's
Voting Rights
ISBN 0-89490-780-8

Thomas Alva Edison
Inventor
ISBN 0-7660-1014-7

Historical American Biographies

ROBERT FULTON

Inventor and Steamboat Builder

James M. Flammang

Enslow Publishers, Inc.
40 Industrial Road   PO Box 38
Box 398   Aldershot
Berkeley Heights, NJ 07922 Hants GU12 6BP
USA   UK
http://www.enslow.com

Library of Congress Cataloging-in-Publication Data

Flammang, James M.
   Robert Fulton : inventor and steamboat builder / James M. Flammang.
      p. cm. — (Historical American biographies)
   Includes bibliographical references and index.
   Summary: Discusses the life and work of the inventor who developed
the steamboat and made it a commercial success.
   ISBN 0-7660-1141-0
   1. Fulton, Robert, 1765–1815—Juvenile literature. 2. Marine
engineers—United States—Biography—Juvenile literature. 3. Inventors—
United States—Biography—Juvenile literature. 4. Steamboats—United
States—History—19th century—Juvenile literature. [1. Fulton, Robert,
1765–1815. 2. Inventors. 3. Steamboats—History.] I. Title. II. Series.
VM140.F9F53   1999
623.8'24'092—dc21
[B]   98-30285
                                                             CIP
                                                              AC

Printed in the United States of America

10 9 8 7 6 5 4 3 2 1

To Our Readers:
All Internet addresses in this book were active and appropriate when we
went to press. Any comments or suggestions can be sent by e-mail to
Comments@enslow.com or to the address on the back cover.

Illustration Credits: Courtesy of the U.S. Naval Academy Museum, pp.
15, 89; Enslow Publishers, Inc., pp. 19, 70, 99; Courtesy of United
States Naval Institute, pp. 103, 104, 112; Gift of Mr. and Mrs. Eli Lilly,
Indianapolis Museum of Art, photograph © 1990 Indianapolis Museum
of Art, p. 58; Eno Collection, Miriam and Ira D. Wallach Division of Art,
Prints and Photographs, The New York Public Library, Astor, Lenox and
Tilden Foundations, p. 95; I. N. Phelps Stokes Collection, Miriam and
Ira D. Wallach Division of Art, Prints and Photographs, The New York
Public Library, Astor, Lenox and Tilden Foundations, p. 110;
Reproduced from the *Dictionary of American Portraits*, Published by
Dover Publications, Inc., in 1967, pp. 6, 32, 34, 39, 53, 75.

Cover Illustration: Corel Corporation (Background—Steamboat);
Courtesy of United States Naval Institute (Inset).

CONTENTS

Robert Fulton

1

SOUND AND FURY: FULTON'S FIRST AMERICAN STEAMBOAT

Endless clouds of dark, dense steam poured from the long, slim boat's smokestack and filled the air around the river. Each time workers stirred the roaring furnace down inside, sparks leaped toward the sky, settling down onto the deck. Now and then, an active spark might even fall dangerously close to onlookers.

Sunday, August 16, 1807, was a hot day in New York City. An eager crowd had lined up along the shoreline of the Hudson River to watch the activities. Robert Fulton's strange steamboat, gliding into the pier to get ready for a long run the next day, made the afternoon seem hotter yet. A fired-up boiler and sizzling steam were not what the audience along the river expected to see on a summer's day.

Few had seen or heard of anything like this before. According to one historian, this "vessel looked like a sawmill mounted on a raft and set on fire."[1]

Steam engines had been invented years earlier. By 1774, James Watt was producing steam engines for sale in England, in partnership with Matthew Boulton. Though Watt is often credited with inventing the steam engine, his ideas built upon the work of others.

Beginning in the late 1700s, steam engines provided power for textile manufacturing plants, which produced wool or cotton fabrics. Those engines helped initiate the Industrial Revolution, but in the United States, not many were used for practical work. Several experimenters had tried to harness steam power for land machines—crude forerunners of the automobile. Yet only a few visionaries ever expected to see such a device out on the water, attempting to propel a boat.

Boats, after all, were moved by the wind. Some used oars. Mixing a sailing ship with an engine did

Was Fulton the First?
Many people believe Robert Fulton "invented" the steamboat. Actually, several men—including at least four in America—had produced an operating steamboat before he did. Inventions often evolve through the work of several people, who might not even be aware of one another. Unlike others, Fulton's steamboat became a commercial success.

not seem normal. Some people even thought it might be the devil's work. They believed it was wrong—perhaps sinful—for people to search for unnatural ways to transport themselves.

A week earlier, on August 9, Fulton had conducted a nearly secret trial of his boat on the lower Hudson River. Even though the paddle wheels were not yet completed, the boat managed to move at three miles per hour on a one-mile journey upriver. A regular sailing craft of Fulton's day might reach that speed, but only with a strong wind at her back. The steamboat, if successful, could do its job regardless of the wind.

Paddle boards installed at first were only three feet long and eight inches wide. Despite the relatively small paddle size, Fulton wrote that the steamboat "beat all the sloops that were endeavoring to stem the tide."[2]

Robert Fulton and his partner in the steamboat venture, Robert Livingston, had learned that the axles, which rotated and transferred motion to the paddle boards, were strong enough for the steam engine to run at full power. This meant paddle boards could be bigger in future boats, for even greater speed.

Fulton's steamboat measured 146 feet long. It had a flat bottom and straight sides, but was considered "graceful" at the bow and stern.[3] Enough fuel was on board to run the engine for eight days.

The exposed, arched-top copper boiler that powered the engine sat on rows of fire brick.

Although the boat had square sails fore and aft, Fulton hoped not to use them. To demonstrate the value of his creation, he wanted the journey to be accomplished strictly by steam power.

For this first voyage, the steamboat had no name. It was simply called "Steamboat," which seemed sufficient, because it was the only one of its kind anywhere in the area—probably the only one in the United States.

Like many other people of his time who came up with new ideas, Fulton was ridiculed by those who refused to believe that a steam-powered boat could operate successfully. Even if it did, they insisted, such a contraption would never be of any real use.

Many joked about "Fulton's Folly," certain that it would fail. As black smoke continued to rise from

Powered by Paddles

In a rowboat, oars push against the water to move the boat forward. The ancient Romans and the Chinese developed ships that used a group of paddles—which worked much like oars—arranged around a wheel. Early paddle-wheel boats were powered by people or oxen. In Fulton's steamboat, a steam engine provided the power to operate the paddles.

the smokestack, some bet that the whole contraption would soon explode.[4] Fulton later complained that while waiting to depart from New York, he "heard a number of sarcastic remarks. This is the way ignorant men compliment what they call philosophers and projectors."[5]

His brief run on the Hudson that Sunday proved successful. A day later, on Monday afternoon, August 17 at one o'clock, Fulton was ready to begin the real journey. He would take his boat upriver to Albany, New York—150 miles away.

Fulton considered the voyage an experiment, but filled the boat with fine food and drink regardless. That was exactly what his guests—mostly well-to-do friends and acquaintances—would expect.

Most folks stayed safely on shore, but forty well-dressed passengers stood aboard this strange and frightening machine. Many were relatives of Livingston. The women wore brightly colored dresses and bonnets. Men wore the fancy ruffled suits that were fashionable at the time. This was hardly the best sort of apparel to withstand the soot and sparks that threatened to drift down onto the boat's deck. The elegant fabrics soon became stained by smoke. Passengers' clothing even began to display tiny burn holes in the fabric.[6]

Fulton's partner, Robert Livingston, chose not to participate in the first portion of the voyage, but intended to join the party later. He did issue invitations to many friends and relatives. Young Helen Livingston wrote to her mother that "Cousin Chancellor" had, "with his usual kindness, invited us to be of the party. He says it will be something to remember all our lives."[7]

A Little-Noticed Event

Only one New York newspaper, *The American Citizen*, published an article about Fulton's trial run. "Mr. Fulton's Ingenious Steam Boat," the paper reported, "sails today . . . to Albany. The velocity of the steamboat is calculated at four miles an hour. [If successful,] it will certainly be a very valuable acquisition to the commerce of the Western States."[8]

One woman who rode on the steamboat during its first voyage wrote to her sister about it. In her view, Fulton's curious-looking boat would probably "frighten some of the Old Dutchmen half out of their wits. They will conclude the enemy is coming in earnest with a machine to blow them all up."[9]

Other people's observations were no less vivid. Some observers

> who saw the boat in the night described her as a "monster moving on the water defying the winds and tide, and belching flames and smoke." Some prostrated themselves and prayed a kind Providence for protection from the approaches of the monster, which was marching on the waters and lighting its pathway with fire.[10]

Of course, there was a logical explanation for the rising spiral of sparks and flames—which would become even more dramatic during later voyages. Fulton's boiler was fueled by coal at first, but he soon switched to pinewood, which was cheaper and more abundant. Pinewood is full of tar, which sparks and smokes when burned. Even during the first voyage, though, whenever the engineer stirred the embers, "a galaxy of sparks ascended."[11]

In a letter to a friend, Fulton himself described those first moments:

> My friends were in groups on the deck. There was anxiety mixed with fear among them. They were silent, sad, and weary. I read in their looks nothing but disaster, and almost repented of my efforts. The signal was given and the boat moved on a short distance and then stopped and became immovable. To the silence of the preceding moment, now succeeded murmurs of discontent, and agitations, and whispers and shrugs. I could hear distinctly repeated—"I told you it was so; it is a foolish scheme; I wish we were well out of it."[12]

At that point, Fulton stood on a platform to address the group, asking that they be patient while he inspected the machinery below deck. After making a minor adjustment, the boat continued on its route.

Once the boat was fully under way, the guests grew calmer. Some even began to sing, turning the experimental excursion almost into a floating party.

In contrast to the joyful, jubilant behavior of his guests, Fulton looked serious. Even "when all seemed achieved," he later wrote, "I was the victim of disappointment."[13] Already, he sensed that criticism might be directed his way after the voyage. Critics might point out that Fulton was not the first person to operate a steamboat. Or, they might suggest that even if a steamboat worked properly, it had no practical value.

For the moment, though, work had to be done to keep the steamboat on a steady course. Because Albany was upstream, the paddles had to push against the natural flow of the river. Progress was slow at first, but the pace increased as the tide changed later in the afternoon.

Fulton's travel companions would have to stay on board for twenty-four hours until the boat reached the town of Clermont—110 miles to the north. Through the afternoon and evening of that first day, they enjoyed fine meals prepared by an expert chef. Business-minded landowners along the way called out congratulations, coming out in their own boats to greet the steamboat.

As night fell, the travelers knew sleep would be difficult. The unfamiliar sound of the engine continued through the night, and the motion of the boat disturbed some passengers. Women went to a makeshift cabin in the stern, while the men stayed on deck.

By morning, many along the way had heard about the venture and came to watch as Fulton's boat steamed past. After their arrival at Clermont on Tuesday afternoon, the travelers spent the night

View of Fulton's steamboat passing the Highlands, painted in 1808.

on land—at the estate of Robert Livingston, Fulton's partner.

During the festivities at Clermont, Livingston announced the engagement of his cousin, Harriet Livingston, to Robert Fulton. Following the announcement, Livingston predicted that the "name of the inventor would descend to posterity as a benefactor to the world."[14]

Some of the remarks from Livingston's relatives were less than kind. John R. Livingston was overheard to say to his cousin, John Swift, that "Bob has had many a bee in his bonnet before now, but this steam folly will prove the worst yet!"[15]

At 9:00 A.M. on the third day of the trip upriver, Fulton's boat continued north toward Albany. This time Robert Livingston rode along, as did his son-in-law, Edward. The governor of New York was among those waiting when the steamboat docked at Albany at 5:00 P.M.

The steamboat's average speed for the 150-mile trip was five miles per hour. That speed was sufficient to beat most sailing vessels of the early nineteenth century.

"She is unquestionably the most pleasant boat I ever went in," wrote one of the passengers. "In her the mind is free from suspense. Perpetual motion authorizes you to calculate on a certain time to land; her works move with all the facility of a clock; and the noise when on board is not greater than that of a vessel sailing with a good breeze."[16]

Back to New York

On Thursday morning at nine o'clock, the steamboat left Albany, heading south on the Hudson. Sightseers had eagerly paid a shilling—a fairly substantial sum in those days—to board the steamboat while it was docked. Yet only a handful of people chose to risk the return journey. Some feared a boiler explosion.[17] The fact that no such mishap had occurred on the trip upriver did not stop the fear of the new, unfamiliar machinery.

At six o'clock, the group arrived for the second time at Livingston's estate at Clermont. Livingston wrote to his son-in-law that at each public landing,

> the sight was amusing. All the people of the town were upon the hills that bound the river, upwards of twenty boats filled with men & women came to meet us having seen us at a great distance coming down. They all made the utmost efforts to keep up with us [but] could not by all their efforts keep near us more than two minutes.[18]

Bright and early the next morning, the boat headed into the last part of its trip, reaching New York City at four o'clock in the afternoon. The southbound trip took thirty hours. Again, this meant an average speed of five miles per hour. Even though the boat was traveling downriver the second time, its speed was no greater than when it moved upriver, against the current.

Although his boat had sails, Fulton never raised them during the journey. He might have except that the wind was blowing in the wrong direction most of the time. If he had, his speed would have been considerably slower.

"She answers the helm [steers] equal to any thing that ever was built," Fulton wrote to Livingston a day after the voyage. "I turned her twice in three times her own length. . . . Yesterday I beat all the sloops that were endeavoring to stem tide with the slight breeze which they had; had I hoisted my sails I consequently should have had all their means added to my own."[19]

An editorial in *The American Citizen* was again the only public notice of Fulton's accomplishment: "We congratulate Mr. Fulton and the country on his success in the steamboat, which cannot fail of being very advantageous. We understand that not the smallest inconvenience is felt in the boat, either from heat or smoke."[20] Of course, those whose clothing had fallen victim to the boat's belching smoke might not have agreed that they had suffered no "inconvenience."

Other newspapers were concentrating on the conspiracy trial of Aaron Burr, the former vice president of the United States. They had no time, it seemed, to pay attention to another "crackpot" inventor.

Despite his concern about criticism, Fulton was more than satisfied with the result of his efforts. He

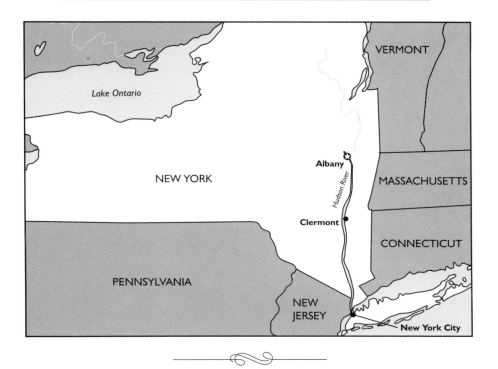

Fulton's first American steamboat left New York City on August 16, 1807. It traveled up the Hudson River to Albany, New York, stopping along the way at Clermont. After an overnight rest, Fulton steamed downriver, back to New York City.

thought the steamboat was "quite perfect—the work of an inventive genius."[21]

Even so, others mistrusted the arrival of steam power. Some feared they would no longer be able to earn a living. Fishermen along the route

> became terrified, and rowed homewards, and they saw nothing but destruction of their fishing grounds, whilst the wreaths of black vapour, and rushing noise of the paddlewheels, foaming with the stirred up waters, produced great excitement amid the boatmen.[22]

Fulton's sense of "disappointment" during the cruise grew stronger, when he heard words of criticism. He expressed his concerns in a letter to a friend, explaining that "[i]t was then doubted if it could be done again, or if done, it was doubted if it could be made of any great value."[23]

Before long, each of those critics would prove to be seriously mistaken. Robert Fulton had not invented the steamboat, but he had demonstrated that the steamboat worked for carrying passengers and cargo. Soon, he would show that it could be put into service as a profitable commercial activity.

2

ONE
TALENTED
BOY

Lancaster County was a sparsely populated region of southern Pennsylvania when Robert Fulton was born on November 14, 1765. Known as Little Britain Township, the area in which he grew up, not far from the Maryland border, was totally rural. Nearby, though, a visitor could find more activity in the growing town of Lancaster itself.

His Scottish father, also named Robert, had immigrated to America from Kilkenny County in Ireland, settling first in Philadelphia. By 1735 he was employed as a tailor in Lancaster—a town that had been established five years earlier. Robert Fulton, Sr., held several village offices in Lancaster over the years, including the post of assistant burgess, and secretary of the Union Fire Office. Because tailoring in a small town could not bring in enough money to support a family, Fulton, Sr., also traded in various goods to earn extra money.[1]

Town life was not wholly satisfying to Robert Fulton, Sr., and his wife, Mary Smith. After meeting in the Lancaster area, the couple had married in 1759, despite the fact that Mary was barely half her husband's age. The daughter of a Scotch-Irish Presbyterian farmer, Mary was "well educated for her time."[2]

They owned a house right on the town square, but Fulton wanted to try something different. So, after years in Lancaster, he decided to try farming, even though he had no experience.

In 1763, Fulton bought 394 acres in Little Britain Township, about thirty miles south of Lancaster. He paid £965 for the property on Conowingo Creek, partly in cash but mostly in the form of a mortgage. Fulton's mortgage amounted to quite a large sum—equivalent to more than one hundred thousand dollars today. Obviously, he would have a substantial debt to pay off.

By the time Robert Fulton, Jr., was born, his parents were settled into a two-story stone farmhouse in Little Britain. They had moved to the farm in the spring of 1765. Robert was the fourth of five children, including three older sisters (Betsy, Belle, and Polly) and a younger brother named Abraham.

Not long after Robert was born, his father's farming venture began to fail. Even though Robert Fulton, Sr., worked hard at tilling his land, the soil was poor for growing crops. Harvests were small—enough to feed the family, but not to earn a profit.

By 1771, creditors foreclosed on the farm and the Fultons were evicted. In the winter of 1771–1772, they returned to Lancaster, with little more than the clothes on their backs.

Robert's father returned to his original occupation: tailoring. Three years later, in 1774, he died, leaving no will, "no doubt because he had little or nothing to leave."[3] The house and furniture had been sold two years before. Robert was only nine years old at the time of his father's death.

A Boy With Ideas

How the widow Fulton managed to support her five children after the death of her husband is not known. Many details of Robert Fulton's childhood are uncertain. As an adult, Fulton himself said and wrote little about his childhood, even in letters to family members.

Some believe, for instance, that at about age fourteen, Robert converted a rowboat into a hand-propelled paddle wheeler, trying it out in a nearby pond. An older friend in the area, Christopher Gumpf, had taken Robert fishing. Unhappy with the performance of Gumpf's boat, some people believe Robert designed and built two paddle wheels for it, operated by hand cranks.[4]

His descendants also believed that Robert created "a small working model of a fishing-boat to be propelled by paddles." Family tradition suggested that such a model was left at an aunt's house and never seen again.[5] Obviously, assembling such a device during his youth would demonstrate a strong indication of early talent for innovation in water transportation. Unfortunately, no real evidence of such a boat exists. In fact, Robert Fulton never mentioned such a thing years later, when he was trying to prove his right to the steamboat idea while applying for patents. If he had really devised a paddle wheel as a teenager, that claim could have given his applications a much stronger basis.

As a boy, Robert is also thought to have invented such items as a rocket that was used in a town celebration. He also may have learned to produce lead pencils and to construct household utensils. Robert also showed a talent for gunsmithing, according to some historians. "He is known to have manufactured an air-gun in the year 1779," his great-granddaughter wrote many years later, "but there is no record of its success."[6] What is known for certain is that at an early age, when most boys preferred to engage in horseplay and physical pursuits, Robert Fulton displayed strong evidence of a busy, inventive mind.

School Days and Dreams

At age eight, before his father's death, Robert Fulton was enrolled in a Quaker school, even though the Fultons were Presbyterians. Before Robert began school, his mother taught him to read and write.

Early in his school years, Robert showed a special talent for drawing. That skill would eventually prove doubly useful, leading him first to a career as an artist, and later yet, helping him develop his inventions and do design work. Fascinated by the colors used by children in their artwork, young Robert began to paint.[7] Before long, it became obvious that his drawings were much better than those of his schoolmates.

The stern teacher, Caleb Johnson, did not make life easy for Robert. Entranced by artwork and tending to daydream a lot, Robert "neglected his studies and was often beaten by the schoolmaster."[8] Corporal punishment was common at that time. Naturally, Robert did not appreciate the custom. "My head is so full of original notions," he allegedly told the schoolmaster, "that there is no vacant chamber to store away the contents of dusty books."[9]

Robert Fulton always seemed to be thinking about projects, drawing things in his mind, or evaluating ideas. Robert even earned the nickname "Quicksilver Bob," partly because his mind changed direction so often and so fast, and partly from his tinkering.[10] Robert is said to have enjoyed experimenting with quicksilver (mercury), a glittery chemical substance that flows in strange ways.

During this time, Robert Fulton was probably exposed to the thoughts of William Henry, a prominent gun maker, inventor, and mechanic. Henry ran the library in Lancaster. Henry's home became an intellectual center of the community, and Robert "undoubtedly had access" to the scientific library, which contained instruments and devices as well as books.[11] Though less famous today than Robert Fulton, Henry became a "steamboat pioneer" himself.[12] As early as 1763, he is thought to have experimented with a boat that contained a steam engine—but the boat sank.[13]

By the time of Robert's boyhood, in the 1770s, Lancaster was becoming quite a lively place. Plenty of travelers passed through this growing town of four thousand inhabitants, on their way west. A boy in Lancaster might observe the hustle and bustle of the busy marketplace. But he also could see such horrific sights as public hangings, right in the town square. Besides that, the American colonists were beginning to demonstrate their displeasure at living under British rule.

Revolution Rears Its Head

By the time Robert was ten years old, the town of Lancaster—and all the towns in the American colonies—were on the brink of a dramatic change. In 1775 the American Revolution was under way.

Some residents preferred things to remain as they were, but most colonists were prepared to struggle to the end in their quest to obtain freedom from England. For years, the Americans had been growing unhappy with their treatment by the government in Great Britain. They had finally decided that the time had come to break away from the British and set up an independent government of their own.

Wartime activities were evident in Lancaster, where citizens could see British sailors captured by American forces. Even though the town was located far from the war front, it served as a major supply

Causes of the American Revolution

Americans had many grievances against King George III and the British Parliament, which controlled the colonies. Several incidents early in the 1770s, including the Boston Tea Party, were protests against Parliament's power to tax the American colonists directly. These events led to the American Revolution. Fighting began in 1775 and lasted until 1781, when the British, under General Charles Cornwallis, surrendered to the American forces of General George Washington.

The Continental Congress, made up of representatives from all thirteen colonies declared American independence from Great Britain in 1776. First established in 1774, the Continental Congress served as the basic governing body for the new nation until it was replaced by the United States Congress in 1789.

depot for General George Washington's Continental Army. No fighting took place there, but soldiers and homeless refugees could be seen on its streets. Lancaster companies manufactured and distributed goods such as rifles, blankets, and clothing for the American troops.

In the fall of 1777, the Continental Congress moved its headquarters to Lancaster for a while. In those autumn months, such famous patriots as Thomas Paine, John Adams, and John Hancock might be seen strolling the streets of Lancaster.

For twelve-year-old Robert Fulton, these were thrilling times. Still, a boy of that age had to begin thinking about a trade. He needed to bring home some money to help his struggling family.

3

THE BUDDING ARTIST

Because Robert Fulton grew up in a poor family, his formal education had ended early. Boys from well-to-do families in the eighteenth century could go on to college, but poor boys had to go to work.

Having displayed such a strong talent for artwork at an early age, becoming a professional artist seemed logical. But how could he make money at his art?

After only a few years of school, young people of Robert Fulton's time often entered apprenticeships. Working under the guidance of an expert for a period of years, they would learn the essentials of a trade or profession. Extensive training would then enable a person to make a decent living.

Here again, the facts about Robert Fulton's preparation are lost. There is no evidence that he received any training or guidance in art in his early teens. As he reached the age when apprenticeships typically began, he was not yet attached to a master in any of the arts or trades.

Most likely, he first learned the basic skills of artwork on his own, taking in a few pennies here and there from his paintings. Even though the town of Lancaster was growing quickly, prospects for a young artist in rural America were not great.

Somewhere between his fourteenth and seventeenth birthdays—perhaps at the age of fifteen—Robert Fulton moved to Philadelphia. One of the largest cities in America, Philadelphia boasted more than forty thousand residents.

Details are uncertain, but many historians believe Robert Fulton served as an apprentice to a silversmith in Philadelphia, learning the trade of working with silver "much against his inclinations."[1]

During his training, Robert learned to melt and shape silver and to engrave designs. While mastering the elements of the silversmith's and jeweler's arts over the next few years, Robert began to specialize in "miniatures." Popular in the late eighteenth century, these were tiny paintings on ivory chips, which were inserted into lockets or bracelets that had been crafted in gold or silver. Miniatures might also be worn inset into rings.

Robert also produced mechanical drawings for clients who wished to manufacture products—including gunsmiths.[2] This experience revealed practical skills that would emerge in his later years, when he turned from art to invention. While working as a painter, Fulton was "known to have drawn plans for machinery, which he submitted to various shops." He also "designed carriages and buildings."[3]

Advertisements for the shop where Fulton worked promoted shoe, knee, and stock buckles, as well as rings, lockets, and brooches. The shop also advertised "hair worked in the neatest manner."[4] This referred to "mourning rings," which bereaved relatives wore following a death in the family. Rings or lockets were decorated with actual hair from the recently deceased.[5] Robert taught himself how to do the intricate weaving of human hair into mourning rings. Strands of hair were used to outline the portrait or whatever subject was to be depicted.

On any day Robert might be seen on the streets of Philadelphia, carrying his tools: a wooden box filled with ivory chips, colored paints, and brushes. Eventually, Robert managed to become a moderately skilled painter of pictures for jewelry. He also painted conventional portraits on canvas.

One of those portraits was thought to be of famous inventor and Founding Father Benjamin Franklin, who could easily have met the young Fulton in Philadelphia. No such portrait exists

Some people believe young Robert Fulton may have met and painted a portrait of the famous inventor and Founding Father Benjamin Franklin while living in Philadelphia.

today, however, so that claim could simply be one more tantalizing rumor about Robert Fulton's early life.

At Last—A Shop of His Own

Seeking independence after his years of training, Fulton opened his own silver shop at Second and Walnut streets, a busy corner in Philadelphia. His shop stood across from the London Coffee House, a center of cultural and political discussion. Although he was hardly one of the top artists in the area, Robert Fulton achieved a "considerable measure of success" in the mid-1780s, according to one biographer.[6] The Philadelphia directory in 1785 listed him as "Fulton, Miniature Painter."[7]

As a young man, Robert Fulton was known as dashing, charming, and handsome. Even though his earnings were not great, he managed to dress well. Skilled in conversation, he was able to make friends easily—a trait that would be even more beneficial in later life. In speech as well as in appearance, Robert Fulton attracted attention easily. As one biographer explained: "His dark eyes imbue with the fire of excitement and energy. . . ."[8] Fulton in his late teens and early twenties was described as a "tall and graceful man . . . with a definite gleam of genius in his face."[9]

The confidence that would mark his adult life was already well established. Fulton "was never one to underestimate his previous achievements or to let fact stand in the way of an impression he wished to make."[10]

A Steamboat in Philadelphia— But Not Fulton's

No evidence suggests that Robert Fulton gave any thought to steamboats during his youth, while training to be an artist. Others were thinking about steam transportation, however. One of them, John Fitch, lived only a few miles from Fulton's Philadelphia shop. Fitch tested a boat on the river there.

Like many other inventors, Fitch was scorned and scoffed at for his early attempts at developing steam travel. A few years later, Fulton, too, would meet his share of critics.

Fulton's America was changing fast as it reached the final days of its struggle for independence from Great Britain. In 1781, the American troops had defeated the British at Yorktown, Virginia, in

During Fulton's youth, others were experimenting with steam-powered boats. Among them was John Fitch, who tested a steamboat of his own near Philadelphia, close to Fulton's shop.

the last big battle of the American Revolution. A year later, work was under way toward signing a treaty to establish American independence from Great Britain, as well as creating a government for the thirteen new United States of America.

Which Way to Turn Next?

Fulton's miniatures and larger artwork demanded patience and painstaking effort, as well as skill. Yet, his results were not necessarily of the highest quality, according to later art critics.

Despite a modest degree of success between the ages of seventeen and twenty-one, the young Fulton has been described as an "artisan" painter, or an "American primitive," rather than a full-fledged professional artist.[11]

To reach the level of a real artist, he would need some serious training and education. He had to develop skills that went well beyond the jeweler's shop and the ability to do conventional portraits of local people. For an education of that sort, a young man would have to travel to Europe, where the serious artists of the time went to study.

4

TO EUROPE

Sometimes, a bout of misfortune leads to abrupt change in a person's life. That is precisely what happened to Robert Fulton, when he was just twenty-one years old.

After developing a bad cough, Fulton desperately needed treatment. Not only were his lungs inflamed, but he began to spit up blood. Doctors could do little for serious ailments in the late eighteenth century. Few medications were available that could help alleviate such a condition.

Exercise and pure air were recommended for breathing problems. Therefore, Fulton was advised to soak in the warm medicinal waters of the springs at Bath, Virginia. Many people believed that the hot spring water had the power to heal a variety of ailments.

Did the waters work? All that is known for sure is that, according to one biographer, "Fulton returned to Philadelphia in splendid health" after spending time in water "hot enough to boil an egg."[1]

A fashionable resort in the country, at high altitude, Bath attracted many famous people, including George Washington, when they needed to relax or recover from an illness. In addition to the healing waters, the resorts had plenty of activities to occupy the invalids' minds, from gambling to theater performances and horse racing.[2]

In the Company of Gentlemen

While at Bath, Fulton became part of a group of gentlemen. Having achieved a modest degree of success in his chosen trade, Fulton realized that he got along quite well with men of the upper classes. For the rest of his life, despite his lack of personal wealth, he would consider himself a "gentleman," too, rather than a worker.

Aware that Fulton would need serious training to develop into a true artist, his new, cultured friends at Bath suggested that he pursue further study in Europe. Only in Europe, they believed, could he develop his skills to a suitable level for serious success.

They advised Fulton to study under Benjamin West. Several of the gentlemen in the area gave

Fulton letters of introduction to the famous West, who lived in London, England.

Born in Pennsylvania in 1738, Benjamin West had begun to draw in the 1750s. As a young man, he had come to Lancaster—Fulton's hometown—to paint portraits of prominent people. Then, West had moved on to Philadelphia, before going to Europe and becoming a world-renowned artist.

Although the two almost certainly never met during West's stay in Lancaster, Robert Fulton might well have been inspired by West's awesome reputation. Many earlier American painters had already gone to study with West in Europe.

After spending time at Bath among the educated and cultured "gentlemen," Fulton returned to Lancaster.[3] He realized that a stay in London would be essential to obtain the training he needed.

Unfortunately, getting there would take more money than Fulton was likely to earn painting

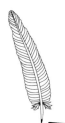

Benjamin West

Traveling first to Italy and, in 1763, to England, West became the "court painter to [King] George III and perhaps the most admired artist in the Western world."[4] West was the first of many American artists to leave his home country to live in Europe. On the other side of the Atlantic Ocean, he became known as the "American Raphael," a reference to the famous classical European artist.[5]

Fulton traveled to Europe, where he would study art under the guidance of the famous Benjamin West.

miniatures. So, Fulton expanded his work to include regular oil paintings and pastels, which brought larger fees.

Fortunately, Fulton had become acquainted with several well-to-do men in the Philadelphia area. These men had taken an interest in Fulton's artistic career. One of them—maybe even several of them—just might be willing to help finance his study abroad.

Mother's Welfare Comes First

Before leaving for Europe, Fulton had one important duty to handle. To make certain that his mother would have a place to live for the rest of her life, he bought her a small farm in Washington County, in western Pennsylvania. The price was £80, equivalent to about $8,500 in today's money.

Although Fulton had been saving a substantial amount from his earnings, artists in the eighteenth century did not earn high incomes. "Documents indicate he borrowed part, if not all, of the £80," wrote one biographer.[6] Not only did Fulton make a down payment of £8 on the farm, but he invested an additional £5 in nearby lots. And he still had enough cash left over to get to England.[7]

Fulton discovered that plenty of affluent people would eagerly dispense money to a deserving young man. Some of those benefactors were content merely to assist Fulton in achieving his goals. Others accepted shares in a new venture, hoping for profits at a later date. Either way, they provided the funds that Fulton, as a gentleman who could not be bothered with taking an ordinary job, was unable to amass himself.

Off to England

Already, Robert Fulton had "acquired an awe-inspiring confidence in his own powers."[8] He had no doubt that he would be successful, once he honed his talents.

In the summer of 1787, Fulton sailed to London. His passage was paid by several Philadelphia merchants. Fulton did not realize it at the time, but he would be spending the next two decades in Europe—first in England and then in France—before returning to his native land.

Although his letters of introduction eased Fulton's entry into Benjamin West's group, becoming a serious artist turned out to be hard work. "Painting requires more study than I at first imagined," he wrote in a letter to his mother.[9] Despite the difficulty, however, Fulton continued to be confident of his own abilities.

Fulton also proved to be "a master at getting on with the great."[10] He kept expanding his circle of friends to include people of prominence. West, in fact, once wrote to Fulton's mother, noting her son's "ingratiating address and manners."[11]

Living first in a coffeehouse for a shilling per week, Fulton moved frequently during his stay in

London. He eventually took rooms among other struggling artists over the next few years.

Not much time passed before Fulton's money began to run out. He had to live frugally, doing without most of life's extra comforts.

It took quite a while, but eventually he began to sell paintings, including portraits of the British nobility. Lord William Courtenay, for one, in the county of Devonshire, commissioned a portrait of himself to be painted by Fulton. For more than a year, Fulton lived as a guest at Powderham Castle, which was owned by Courtenay.

A letter dated July 25, 1788, from Fulton's friend George Sanderson to Mary Fulton, commended her son's progress "in the liberal Art of Painting." Sanderson noted that Fulton had influential friends, won by "his personal accomplishments and prudent behavior."[12]

Fulton wrote to his mother in 1789, informing her that his paintings had been admitted to the Royal Academy of Arts. Founded in 1768, the Royal Academy held annual exhibitions, aiming to improve the status of artists.

Actually, Fulton's claim was premature. Not until 1791 was one of his portraits exhibited at the academy. Four other pictures went to the less-demanding Society of Artists during that same year.

Two years later, two more paintings went on display at the prestigious Royal Academy. That was a high honor for an artist from the other side of the Atlantic Ocean—or for any aspiring artist.

"What was most conspicuous in his character," wrote Fulton's first biographer, Cadwallader D. Colden, "was his calm constancy, his industry, and that indefatigable patience and perseverance which always enabled him to overcome difficulties."[13]

"Nature had made him a gentleman," said Colden of the slender, six-feet-tall Robert Fulton, "and bestowed upon him ease and gracefulness. . . . His features were strong, and of a manly beauty . . . his temper was mild, and his disposition lively."[14] Fulton was also described as "fond of society, which he always enlivened by cheerful, cordial manners, and instructed or pleased by his sensible conversation."[15]

One of the men who sat for a portrait by Fulton was Lord Charles Stanhope, who closely followed technical advances of the day. Stanhope was particularly interested in navigation and water transportation, and Fulton would use that acquaintance later.

Artists Need More Than Confidence

Back in Lancaster, Fulton's jewelry work had been rated good, though not great. Here in London, too, his paintings were not considered inspired.

Fulton was able to earn a modest income by painting, but not much more than that. "Many, many a silent, solitary hour have I spent in the most unnerved study," he wrote, "anxiously pondering how to make funds to support me till the fruits of my labors should suffice to repay them."[16] By sticking to portrait painting, he eventually realized, his success would be limited. He would probably never achieve the critical recognition that was as important to an artist as money.

Even a brief visit to France, to study the works of the masters, did not provide sufficient inspiration. As one historian noted, however, Fulton "studied great paintings not so much to improve his technique as to improve his earning power."[17]

Being a man "whose ambitions never knew any bounds," Fulton would have to seek his fame and fortune elsewhere.[18] Fortunately, by then, Robert Fulton had other prospects in mind. He had taken an interest in invention, starting with new ideas for water transportation in rural England.

Did Robert Fulton have any notions as yet about the steamboat? Nothing in his writings suggests that he did. On November 6, 1788, however, James Rumsey was granted a steamboat patent. An innkeeper and carpenter in Bath, Virginia, Rumsey had worked on canal design and developed a steamboat in the late 1780s.

Sometime during 1789, Rumsey described his work to William West, a fellow pupil of Fulton's at Benjamin West's studio.[19] Could the seeds of the steamboat have been planted by an idle conversation among artists in England?

5

ABANDONING ART FOR TECHNOLOGY

Not long after having his portraits exhibited at the Royal Academy, Robert Fulton began to steer his career away from art. Rather than struggle further in a field that would never reward him sufficiently, he considered other ways to earn a living and a way to make a difference in the world.

Early in the 1790s, his attention gradually turned to technical matters and inventions. Portrait work slipped into second place. Benjamin West himself observed that "doubting his success" as a painter, Fulton "turned his attention to mechanics."[1]

Although Fulton would continue to paint for the rest of his life, art ceased to be his career. Any painting he might do in later life would be done for pleasure, not for money.

Fulton took a particular interest in transportation and in the problems of developing a ship that could move under its own power, without sails or oars. He learned, for instance, of a recently devised single-paddle boat. He also followed the developments of several inventors in the field of steam power.

The Canal Question

Before turning to steam engines, however, he focused his attention on the canal boats that carried goods throughout Great Britain. The first canals had been built in the 1760s and 1770s. Though some of the early builders were scorned, some of their ventures began to make enormous profits.

"I have laid aside my panels," Fulton wrote in a letter home in September 1796, "and have not painted a picture for more than two years, as I have little doubt but canals will answer my purposes much better."[2] From this point forward, Fulton used his talents primarily for illustrations and drawings of mechanical devices.

Motor vehicles and railroads did not yet exist, so most merchandise was transported by boat. A network of canals throughout the country was essential to commerce. Horses walking alongside could pull boats through such canals.

Political leaders naturally welcomed new ideas for improving the movement of goods from one town to another. Fulton believed that a system of small canals "would bring universal prosperity."[3]

Technical issues were just one part of the equation. Robert Fulton, in the words of his great-granddaughter, "viewed the possibilities of canal navigation as contributing to the best form of political economy for any nation which would adopt it. He calculated the profits to be derived, the expenses incident to the development of his plan." In his view, a vast network of canals, "like arteries of the body, would unite all parts of the country."[4] If canals proved valuable to commerce in England, they could also be useful in the United States.

By 1794, Fulton had fully accepted his failure as a serious painter. In that same year, he received a British patent for the use of a double inclined plane in canals. Fulton's design used a set of rails, working with pulleys in a wooden framework to haul boats uphill.

This system was designed to replace locks, which were necessary when water levels differed between one waterway and another. Without some system of equalization, allowing for the differences between levels, boats could not travel through a canal system. An inclined plane was one way for boats to be raised and lowered to match the water level of the adjoining waterway.

As it turned out, an inclined-plane system had already been developed and found to be flawed. In September 1793, Fulton sent Lord Stanhope a

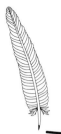

Canals and Locks

English roads in the eighteenth century were nearly impassable, barely fit for horses. Canals became the preferred way to move people and cargo between towns and cities. To allow canal boats to follow hilly terrain, locks were needed.

A boat could sit in a closed-off section on one side of the closed lock. Water was pumped in. The boat slowly rose, to meet the level of the water in the adjoining canal segment. When the lock opened, the boat could simply move forward again.

sketch of his own inclined-plane system. He also explained that he had ideas for a steamboat. Stanhope replied that the inclined-plane concept was not new, but he would like to hear more about Fulton's steamboat notion.[5] Several other inventors had devised steamboats by this time, including John Fitch, James Rumsey, and the Marquis de Jouffroy in France, but none had proved successful.

Lord Stanhope was himself an advanced thinker on scientific subjects. He had been working on canals and powered ships for some years. Stanhope had even patented a steamboat concept. Fulton sent Stanhope some crude steamboat drawings of his own, with a rudimentary paddle wheel, but nothing developed at this time. He continued to concentrate on canals.

Fulton's Inclined Plane

Canals were essential to commerce in England, but the locks used to permit boats to travel uphill and downhill were cumbersome. To replace the locks, Robert Fulton devised a system of inclined planes. A boat would sit on a carriage, which rode an inclined rail. A parallel rail held a second carriage, which would be filled with water. As the weight of the water carriage increased, the boat would gradually move up the incline, through use of pulleys and ropes. Fulton was not the first to attempt an inclined-plane system, which saw use in America years after his death.

Two years later, in 1796, Fulton wrote *A Treatise on the Improvement of Canal Navigation*. In addition to descriptions of many mechanical devices, the book included seventeen illustrations. Of course, that was not a difficult task for Fulton, with his extensive art training. Designs for aqueducts and bridges were included.

Fulton was nothing if not thorough. He envisioned a complete plan for canal networks, not just a simple idea. In his book, Fulton described a comprehensive system of inland transportation, using small-wheeled boats that would follow a network of narrow canals. Such a system could be implemented throughout the world, solving the problems of inland transportation. Inclined planes could be used to make the voyages possible. Fulton also proposed to arrange his boats in a group, "attaching a string of ten to a single horse."[6]

Robert Fulton: Self-Styled Engineer

By this time, Fulton referred to himself as a "civil engineer," listing that personal title on his book's title page. Despite the fact that he had had no formal training in engineering, Fulton's words were thoughtfully considered. He even sent copies of his treatise to George Washington, now president of the United States, and to other notable men.

Traveling around England, Fulton had seen poor farmland in the areas of Devon and Cornwall, in western England. Not much fertile soil was available for tilling, but if fertilizer could be transported easily to these regions, this marginal land might become a lot more productive.

His canal plan called for cast-iron aqueducts, in a network that would encompass all of England. Fulton even designed a digging machine to construct the canals. Such a device could scoop out earth, forming channels for water to flow in canals or aqueducts.

Actually, the digging machine was a "crude and impracticable apparatus," according to one biographer.[7] Fulton did not even mention it in his treatise.

Despite his continual need for money, Fulton never sought a job at any canal project. He continued to call himself a "gentleman," and "gentlemen did not in those days serve as subordinates."[8]

Already, Robert Fulton had recognized that an

invention did not have to be wholly original to be valuable. Instead, it could be a compilation of old ideas or an improvement upon someone else's idea. As long as it worked, who cared how it was developed?

Fulton believed that advances in technology should be viewed as improvements, not inventions. He wrote:

> [The] component parts of all new machines may be said to be old; but it is that nice discriminating judgement, which discovers that a particular arrangement will produce a new and desired effect, that stamps the merit. . . . The mechanic should sit down among levers, screws, wedges, wheels, etc., like a poet among the letters of the alphabet, considering them as the exhibition of his thought, in which a new arrangement transmits a new idea to the world.[9]

While writing his *Treatise on the Improvement of Canal Navigation*, Fulton established a friendship with Robert Owen, a manufacturer and socialist reformer who lived in Manchester. In later years, Owen would become known for his creation of a utopian community in America, at New Harmony, Indiana.

Fulton and Owen became partners in December 1794. Fulton asked Owen for funds to work on a canal project near Gloucester, using his digging machine. Owen offered the money in exchange for a half interest in the project. In 1797, Fulton was able to pay Owen back, at least partially, by selling some of his own share.

Whatever its merits, no one in the British government was ready to make a decision to adopt such a canal system. Not until the early 1820s would a variant of Fulton's idea be adopted.

Fulton also advocated that a canal be constructed in the United States, between Philadelphia and Lake Erie. He recommended the project to President George Washington, but the American government failed to follow his advice, despite great interest in canals in the United States.

These rejections must have disappointed Fulton, but he was never the sort to give up. Always confident, despite the comments of scoffers, he was ready to move on to other projects. Surely, one of them would turn out to be his great success. Just one

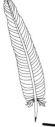

Utopian Movements

Robert Owen (1771–1858), a British social reformer and cotton manufacturer, was one of the best known founders of the utopian movement. His Lanark cotton mills were set up not as an ordinary manufacturing area, but as a model community—a "utopia." The name came from a fictional republic, called *Utopia*, in a novel by Sir Thomas More. Eventually, the name was used to identify any ideal state. Utopians believed in social harmony and perfect order. Owen established such a community near Glasgow, Scotland, and another in New Harmony, Indiana, in the United States. Neither community survived for long.

While in Europe, Fulton formed a friendship with socialist reformer
Robert Owen, who became Fulton's partner in a canal operation
in 1794.

big idea was all he might need to become recognized throughout the world.

Many Inventions, But Little Success

Not all of his inventions and improvements had to do with waterways. During the 1790s, Fulton developed a machine to cut and polish marble, for use in furniture inlays. He designed another machine that would spin flax fiber into yarn. Modifying that design a little, he came up with a device that could twist hemp into sturdy rope.

None of his devices caught on, but they did earn him some recognition as an inventor. In 1794 the British Society of Arts and Commerce awarded him an honorary medal for his invention of the marble-sawing device.

Robert Fulton stood ahead of rival inventors in one crucial respect. He did not have to build a series of models of his ideas. Because of his artistic training, he simply made sketches. Then, he could pick the best one to be used as a basis for the final model. That process saved a lot of time and effort.

As he observed boats and ships in England, Fulton began to concentrate more on the idea of powered boats. Sailing ships dotted the seas all over the world in the eighteenth century. Sailing craft also plied the lakes and rivers of nearly every nation. Subservient to the whims of the wind, sailboats had obvious limitations. Anyone could see that a better method of propulsion would be beneficial, but how could it be done?

As early as 1793, Fulton had been thinking about the use of steam engines in boats. James Watt's steam engine, available since 1774, had seen considerable use in manufacturing plants, but not in boats.

Along the way, Fulton undoubtedly became aware of the work of James Rumsey and John Fitch, among others. Each of these men had been working on the idea of steamboat travel. Before producing his first steamboat, Fulton "knew very nearly all that had been done in the way of experiments, and his ability lay in selecting those features that were of value and bringing them together."[10]

Others had been working on a boat with a single paddle, powered by a steam engine. Fulton's own experiments suggested instead the use of a group of revolving paddles, mounted at the stern of the ship.

James Watt and the Steam Engine
Born in Scotland in 1736, James Watt trained as an instrument maker and surveyed canals. By 1757, he was studying the properties of steam as a motive force. A steam engine already existed, but Watt improved the design by devising a separate condenser for the steam. In 1774, he formed a partnership with Matthew Boulton to build steam engines. Watt was the first person to use the term *horsepower*, comparing the power produced by an engine to the power of a horse pulling, to specify the potential output of an engine.

Fulton was already in contact with the British firm of Boulton & Watt, a supplier of steam engines. Why couldn't the two ideas—steam power and paddle wheels—be combined into a workable, steam-powered ship?

"Fulton's teeming brain threw out idea after idea for possibly valuable invention," wrote one biographer, including his canal-cutting machine and "a new method of tanning." Nevertheless, at the age of thirty-two, Fulton "had succeeded at nothing."[11]

Lack of real success as a painter was the first blow. The fact that his prized canal system earned no backers added to the disappointment. Even so, Robert Fulton was not about to give up.

He thought of another place to go. Getting no satisfaction from the British, Fulton sailed to France in the spring of 1797. Perhaps he would have better luck there, convincing the political leaders of that country to try out his transportation ideas.

Meeting the Barlows

Fulton's arrival in France was delayed for three weeks at the port of Calais, due to trouble with his passport. Travel could be difficult at this time, because of ongoing tensions between France and England, though a respite from hostilities had taken place recently. Since 1789, under the battle cry of "liberty, equality, fraternity," participants in the French Revolution had been fighting for a constitutional government and the downfall of the aristocracy. The battles reached beyond France, encompassing England and the rest of Europe.

Fulton had applied for a passport, but left England without it, believing the document would be waiting for him at Calais. After remaining in that city for three weeks, he simply went on to Paris without a passport.

Paris is "gay and joyous," Fulton wrote in July 1797. "I have good reason to believe there will be good encouragement to men of genius."[12] Never a modest man, Fulton had no hesitation about declaring himself to be one of the geniuses of the world.

Once in France, Fulton met two men who would have a huge impact on his life: Joel Barlow, an American who had moved to France and become a consul; and Robert Livingston, who would later become Fulton's partner in the steamboat operation in New York State.

Born in poverty in America, not unlike Fulton, Joel Barlow was a celebrated poet, publisher, and author. An honorary citizen of France, he also ranked as a statesman and philosopher. After occupying a room at the same hotel as Barlow, Fulton soon moved into the Barlow home.

"A warm friendship at once sprung up between the younger inventor and Mr. Barlow," wrote one of Barlow's biographers, despite an eleven-year difference in their ages. "The relations between the two men of genius during this period were those of

Robert Fulton painted this portrait of his friend and mentor, Joel Barlow, in 1805. The two men met in Paris, France, where Fulton went to work on his steamboat.

Joel Barlow: Statesman, Poet, Mentor

Born in Redding, Connecticut, in 1754, Joel Barlow earned a bachelor's degree from Yale University. After graduating, Barlow taught school, ran a business, published a journal, and became a lawyer. In 1788 he left for Europe and stayed there for seventeen years. During part of that period, he served as a consul and helped establish treaties.

Because of his aid to rebels during the French Revolution, Barlow was the only American who also held French citizenship at that time. Without Barlow's friendship and assistance, Robert Fulton might have had a far more difficult time putting his steamboat ideas into practice.

father and son."[13] Throughout Fulton's work over the next few years, Joel Barlow would serve as a mentor and advisor. He encouraged and helped finance Fulton's ventures and helped instill an aversion to militarism. Barlow even gave the younger man a nickname. In most of his letters, Barlow referred to Fulton as "Toot." Fulton also developed a special friendship with Ruth, Barlow's wife, and often accompanied her on out-of-town journeys.

Although Fulton had regularly corresponded with his mother and other family members during his years in England, he had never returned home for a visit. Mary Fulton, Robert's mother, died in Pennsylvania in 1799, without having seen her eldest son since his departure from America thirteen years earlier.

6

A PRIMITIVE SUBMARINE

After arriving in Paris in June 1797, Fulton planned to continue work on canal projects. Even if the British had rejected his ideas, perhaps the French would consider them more promising.

Paris was an exciting, open-minded city, a place for fun. That was quite a difference from London, where everything tended to be more formal. Partygoers, for instance, danced the "daring" waltz in Paris, in which "partners put their arms around each other," rather than the prim and methodical minuet that was seen at British gatherings, in which little more than fingertips ever touched.[1]

In a letter, Fulton described the city as "gay and joyous, as if there were no war at all."[2] In fact, however, hostilities between England and France had again become intense.

Though intending to remain for only six months, Fulton would stay in France for seven years. By the time he departed in 1806, not one, but two of his greatest inventions would be demonstrated successfully.

Can People Travel Like Fish?

Finding little interest from the French government in canal projects, Fulton continued to think about steam power for ships. But that project would have to wait. Soon, he turned his attention to a new idea: the intriguing concept of submarines and their potential uses in warfare. Opposed to war himself, Fulton saw the submarine as a way to bring military conflicts to a halt. In his eyes, it could be what one biographer called "a curious machine for mending the system of politics."[3] If one nation had submarines on hand, Fulton thought, it might make other nations too fearful to declare war at all.

For centuries, people had wondered whether it might be possible for humans to function underwater, like a fish. The problems seemed insurmountable. How could they breathe? How could an undersea vessel be maneuvered? Would a compass operate below the surface of the water? How would the occupants of such a vessel know what was happening above?

Ever since the seventeenth century, if not earlier, experimenters had been tinkering with the idea of a submersible vessel. An American, David Bushnell, had already invented a "plunging boat" some twenty years earlier. Bushnell's boat was able to descend beneath the water's surface but had not performed well. Named the *American Turtle*, just seven and a half feet long, it looked like a fat cigar and could hold only one person. Able to submerge for thirty minutes, the craft "floated, bobbing, just below the surface with only its small, primitive conning tower exposed."[4] Bushnell's small-scale submarine was able to maneuver below an enemy's ship but failed to sink it in a trial run.[5] Fulton envisioned a larger vessel, able to carry several people, and had great hopes for its success.

During the Napoleonic era, in which French General Napoléon Bonaparte assumed power and established a military dictatorship in France, conflict between the British and the French disrupted trade. Warfare took place largely at sea. During hostile times, ships were unable to carry goods between the two nations. Fulton wanted to see free seas restored. He believed submarines could make conventional navy ships essentially worthless. More important, he intended to demonstrate to the French government that a submarine could destroy British warships.

Despite his emphasis on the machinery of war, Fulton's intentions were unbiased. He did not necessarily support the French politically. In fact, one biographer noted that despite offering to create weapons for European nations, Fulton "always remained loyal to his native land," the United States.[6]

Fulton acknowledged the dangers of submarines, but he sought to limit war and piracy. He wanted to see world peace in his lifetime. He thought the submarine would be the answer.

Such a ship could sneak along beneath the sea, move beneath the hull of an opposing ship, plant a bomb that would explode later, and then retreat unnoticed. A submarine would be so deadly, Fulton believed, that opposing nations would renounce war for good, afraid to fight against such an awesome weapon. If all went well, Fulton could bring about world peace and make a name for himself—both at the same time.

Some people considered Fulton's belief that the existence of a superweapon could result in world peace naive, if not foolish. Robert Fulton was convinced that his view was correct. On December 12, 1797, several months after his arrival in France, Fulton sent a proposal to France's government for a submersible ship that could destroy the British Navy.[7]

Panorama: An Alternate Path

While working to develop his submarine, Fulton turned to a completely different endeavor. In London he had come across a panorama—a large dome with pictures displayed on the inside. Movies

The Ultimate Weapon
Can an awful weapon really lead to peace? Fulton believed his submarine could result in a peaceful world. It would be so awesome that nations would be afraid to go to war. In a 1799 letter, Fulton predicted that availability of his submarine would lead nations to put aside their hostilities and behave peacefully.

would not be invented for another century, but people still craved entertainment. They flocked to see the panorama, earning a lot of money for its British owner.

Fulton saw no reason that he should not enjoy similar success in Paris. In 1799 he took out a ten-year patent for a panorama. He then set up a dome on Boulevard Montmarte. It depicted a devastating fire in Moscow, Russia, which had destroyed that city a decade earlier.

Unlike most of Fulton's projects, this one made him money. Profits from the panorama could give him funds for navigational work.[8] He sold the patent after eight months but continued to get a percentage of the receipts.

Fulton's First Underwater Trial

An eager crowd gathered along the Seine River in Paris, on June 13, 1800. Fulton had invited a group of government officials and dignitaries to witness a momentous event. Because of the location of the

Panorama—The IMAX of the Eighteenth Century
There might not have been movies or television in the late eighteenth century, but people still wanted to have fun. For that reason, panoramas became very popular in England and France. Some panoramas could be unrolled, so people could see them without moving. More often, people stood inside a large circular structure and viewed a huge painting of some historical subject, which covered the entire surface around them. A viewer had to turn all the way around to see the whole thing.

submarine's first trial run, some were able to watch the festivities in comfort, from box seats positioned along the river.

Unlike most of Fulton's projects, the "plunging ship" had been built with his own funds, largely earned from the panorama. Work began at the shop of Auguste Charles Périer. Blacksmiths had followed Fulton's own drawings, heating metal in a forge and hammering it into shape.

Equipped with the customary sail, the boat was twenty-four and a half feet long, constructed in an elongated oval shape. A bubble-shaped tower sat atop the hull.

Fulton and his chief assistant, Nathaniel Sargent, approached the primitive submarine in a rowboat.

To make the ship ready to submerge, the mast and sail were folded down. Spectators stared as Fulton opened the hatch of the tower, and the two men squeezed themselves down inside. Stares soon turned to amazement as the ship moved toward the center of the river, halted, and then disappeared beneath the surface, leaving no more than a stream of bubbles.

Minutes passed. More minutes went by. Were the men alive? Was the "plunging ship" still in its original location? Had eagerness turned to tragedy?

Their questions were answered after forty-five minutes, by a flurry of bubbles reaching the water's surface—quite a distance from the spot where the submarine had submerged. Soon, the bubble top of the submarine burst through the surface. Once the vessel was fully afloat, the hatch opened, and a jubilant Robert Fulton climbed out to greet the crowd.

He had demonstrated that a submarine could work. Not only could its occupants breathe under water, but the vessel could be steered and propelled forward.

A submarine first had to deal with two major, obvious problems: how to get it to sink, and later, how to resurface. To make the boat drop below the water's surface, water had to be pumped into storage tanks in its hollow keel. To rise up again, a pump simply extracted water from the tanks.

While below the surface, too, the occupants needed a supply of air to breathe. For its initial trials, only the air available within the ship was used for breathing. Candles provided illumination inside. But because candles depleted the oxygen in the air as they burned, they limited the potential duration of any submersion.

A delegation sent by Napoléon Bonaparte, France's leader since 1799, watched the plunging-boat demonstration on the Seine. Napoléon wanted to extend the reach of his empire, entering into war as needed in his attempt to gain additional territory.

One observer, Pierre Forfait, reported to Napoléon that

> everything that could be desired was completely achieved. The boat submerged and rose again with great facility. The men who operated it remained inside the boat for forty-five minutes, without renewing the air and when they disembarked no alterations could be seen in their faces.[9]

For its second trial, in late July 1800, Fulton towed the copper submersible ship, named the *Nautilus*, farther up the Seine River to Rouen, about eighty miles from Paris. This time, a three-man crew went down.

Fulton described the submersion himself, saying they began by "plunging to the depth of 5 then 10 then 15 and so on, to 25 feet, . . . At that depth I remained one hour with my three companions and two candles burning without experiencing the least inconvenience."[10] Fulton estimated that the plunging boat's interior volume was 212 cubic feet. That would be "sufficient Oxygen to nourish 4 men and two small candles 3 hours."[11]

In a letter, Fulton reported that he managed to stay below the surface for four hours and twenty minutes. He also explained that he had succeeded in each of these goals:

> To sail like a common boat. To obtain air and light. To plunge and rise perpendicular. To turn to the right and left at pleasure. To steer by the compass under water. To renew the Common Volume of air with facility. And to augment the respirable air by a reservoir which may be obtained at all times.[12]

That was quite a feat for a failed artist, who had yet to earn from his inventive efforts.

Over the next few months, Fulton made improvements to the *Nautilus*. So occupants could see inside while underwater, without using candles, a tiny airtight window was installed. Though only an inch and a half in diameter, it provided enough light for Fulton to see his watch at a depth of twenty-five feet.[13] The submarine now had a periscope, too, rotated by a hand crank.

Fulton also devised a better way to supply oxygen to the crew. While below the surface, the occupants breathed from tanks of compressed air. In theory, at least, they would be able to breathe for as long as ten hours.

St. Aubin, a member of the French tribunate, described Fulton's concept in a newspaper report:

> The diving boat will . . . contain eight men and provision for twenty days, and will be of sufficient strength and power to enable him to plunge 100 feet under water if necessary. He has contrived a reservoir of air, which will enable eight men to remain under water eight hours. When the boat is above water it has two sails, and looks just like a common boat. [Fulton] proved that the compass points as correctly under water as on the surface, and that while under water the boat made way at the rate of half a league [approximately two miles] an hour.[14]

Bombs Away?

Developing a submarine that could travel underwater was just part of the project. Fulton also turned his attention toward the weapons that it might deliver. Such a ship had to be capable of destroying an enemy vessel by placing an explosive device against its hull or by sending a "torpedo" in its direction, underwater. "It is this Bomb which is the Engine of destruction," wrote Fulton's great-granddaughter years later.[15]

In the summer of 1801, Fulton's ship succeeded in destroying a large sloop at the port of Brest. That demonstration "was attested by numerous spectators, and public approval was not lacking."[16]

One problem went unsolved. How could the submarine move adequately while underwater? After all, it was operated merely by hand cranks, which drove a propeller at the front. No one

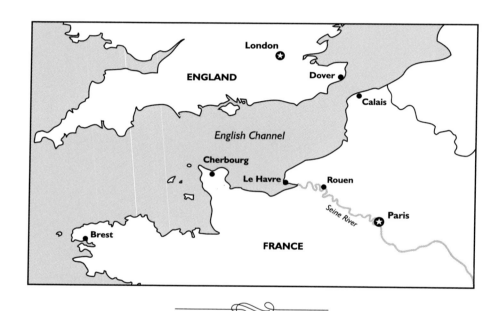

In 1800 Fulton experimented with his Nautilus *submarine on the Seine River at Paris, Rouen, and Le Havre, France. In 1801 his submarine destroyed a sloop at Brest.*

thought seriously of using any sort of motor at this time.

A newspaper report after the trial at Brest on July 26, 1801, noted that "with the exertion of one hand only," the submarine's helmsman "could keep her at any depth he pleased." But in seven minutes, the boat went just five hundred yards.[17]

In the open sea, Fulton's submarine was simply too slow, unable to propel itself forward at a sufficiently rapid rate to overtake a pair of British enemy ships. Actually, Fulton faced a different obstacle when he attempted to approach two British ships— a trial that added an element of danger from real adversaries. Before his *Nautilus* could submerge and come close, the ships simply pulled up their anchors and set sail, leaving Fulton and his crew far behind. The British evidently had been warned of his intentions to cause damage and took precautions to prevent the attack.[18]

On that occasion, Fulton's submarine was gone for three days. While waiting for the tide to change, Fulton intended to submerge for as long as six hours.[19] During that period, the crew breathed air supplied through a metal tube, extended above the water's surface.

Napoléon Bonaparte, the emperor of France, became impressed with the concept, but not soon enough. The French failed to hire Fulton for such a project, and the idea faded away.

Some Frenchmen even thought the notion of warfare by submarine would be dishonorable. They insisted warfare was improper if conducted by stealth. Civilized warriors were expected to remain out in the open, not approach the enemy from beneath the sea.

While in France, Fulton had met Robert Livingston, who would become his future partner for steamboat ventures in the United States. Livingston, appointed United States minister to France in the fall of 1800, was an ardent advocate of the steamboat idea. In fact, he helped develop a working steamboat himself. Measuring only twenty-five feet in length, the *Little Juliana* operated successfully in New York Harbor in 1804.[20]

No less important, Livingston had obtained an exclusive right to create a steamboat service back in the United States. Who better than Robert Fulton to develop the ship that would handle that job?

7

FULTON'S FIRST STEAMBOATS

R obert R. Livingston arrived in Paris late in 1801, to serve as the United States minister to France. By that time, he had learned of Fulton's reputation as an inventor. The two men "accidentally met" early in 1802, according to Fulton.[1] Livingston indicated a willingness to invest a substantial sum of money to construct a practical steamboat.

Livingston had been appointed to his current post by President Thomas Jefferson. Twenty years older than Fulton, Livingston was well known in American politics, previously serving as President George Washington's secretary of state. Livingston had even served on the committee that wrote the Declaration of Independence.

On October 10, 1802, Fulton and Livingston entered into a formal partnership to develop the steamboat. The partners agreed that Fulton would design and produce a steamboat, which could eventually be used on American waterways. They planned to begin with the New York-to-Albany run.

Specifically, the Fulton-Livingston agreement stipulated "that a passage boat moved by the power of a Steam Engine," built at New York, would "run 8 miles an hour in stagnate water and carry at least 60 passengers."[2]

Steamboats had been on Livingston's mind for quite a while. Despite a lack of artistic or mechanical skills, he saw himself as an inventor.[3] In 1798, prior to his move to France, he had obtained a twenty-year monopoly for steamboat service in New York State. Rights would be granted only if Livingston produced an actual operating steamboat within one year.

After making the agreement with Fulton, Livingston was able to secure an extension on his monopoly. He would be allowed more time to get a steamboat ready for service in New York. To obtain the extension, Livingston had to agree that a boat would be completed in a specified time, and could achieve a certain speed—at least four miles per hour.

Convinced that someone else might develop a workable steamboat before long, Livingston wanted to be prepared to start such a business as soon

Robert Livingston, President Jefferson's minister to France, would become Fulton's partner and close friend.

as possible. Livingston was more interested in steamboat travel on the Hudson River than submarines in Europe. Fulton preferred to work on both projects but "could never muster the same passion for the steamboat that he had for the submarine."[4]

Joel Barlow believed he could obtain "funds without any noise" if Fulton wanted to rely less on Livingston.[5] Barlow also predicted that Fulton could get as much money as he wanted for further development in the United States if the first steamboat trial proved successful.[6]

Before returning to the United States to take advantage of Livingston's monopoly in New York, Fulton had to have a steamboat. The two men could not wait any longer to get started. Fulton needed to experiment with steam power right where he was at the moment. Therefore, he concentrated his attention on the possibility of demonstrating a steamboat in France.

That ability to improve upon prior efforts at creating a steamboat turned out to be the secret of Robert Fulton's success. As one biographer put it, "Fulton took the products of the genius of other mechanics, and set them at work in combination, and then applied the already known steam-boat in his more satisfactorily proportioned form, to a variety of useful purposes, and with final success."[7]

Like other inventors before him, Fulton came from the artisan class. He knew how to use tools.

How a Steam Engine Works
Unlike an automobile engine, a steam engine is an "external combustion" device. Its working fluid (steam) is generated in a separate boiler. Heat from burning fuel boils water, turning it into steam. Steam enters the engine itself through valves. As the steam expands due to pressure, a piston is forced outward, then back again, within a large cylinder of the engine. A crankshaft device converts the back-and-forth movement of the piston into rotary motion.

But he also was able to read and understand the scientific theories of water propulsion. Combining those abilities with the availability of Livingston's money turned Robert Fulton into a "serious contender" for steamboat success.[8]

Robert Fulton Works on His Steamboat

After agreeing to Livingston's partnership offer, Fulton began to draw plans. For the American operation, Fulton initially considered a boat that was only ninety feet long and six feet wide. If all went well, it would be capable of moving at eight miles per hour upstream (against the river current). Such a boat could make the run between Albany and New York City in eighteen to twenty hours. If it could carry fifty passengers, the steamboat might clear almost two hundred dollars per trip, or four dollars per passenger.

Fulton also considered a longer boat, capable of holding more people. If a steamboat of increased size could travel at twelve miles per hour, he reasoned, the partners could charge a lower fare and still earn handsome profits. Fulton believed that "it seems advisable to go quick, carry cheap, and thus avoid the competition of boats with sails or carriages."[9] As the steamboat came into existence, however, the higher speed that he saw as a goal would prove to be more difficult to achieve than he had imagined.

Auguste Périer, an expert shipbuilder, had helped Fulton build the *Nautilus* submarine. Now, Périer offered his services for development of the steamboat. Fulton also employed Etienne Calla, a mechanical engineer and instrument maker, to assist with the creation.

Périer and Calla worked on the engine, while Fulton pondered the boat's paddle wheels and hull. Fulton knew that the hull needed to be very strong. Only then could it withstand the incessant movement of a steam engine with its huge piston moving back and forth, over and over again.

After considering various methods of propulsion, including a pulsating tail that mimicked a fish's movement, Fulton decided on paddle wheels. Two properties of water were vital to his thinking. The first was that the resistance of water tends to slow down a moving object. Therefore, the hull had to be streamlined. The second property was that water eventually gives way to a moving object. So, paddles had to have sufficient thrust to propel the boat, not just to spin freely. Without a full understanding of these basic principles, a successful steamboat would be difficult, if not impossible, to build.

A Scale Model

By the summer of 1802, Etienne Calla had built a model for Fulton. Four feet long and two feet wide, it was driven by two clockwork springs. With the model, Fulton could easily test various types of paddles and propellers. The most effective system, he discovered, made use of flat, boardlike paddles attached to a chain.[10]

After experimenting with the scale model, in late 1802 Fulton "gave the preference to a wheel on each side of the model."[11] Even after he decided to use paddle wheels, Fulton needed to determine how big they should be. He also had to decide how many paddles each wheel should hold. To get the most efficient result, a lot of calculations and experiments were required.

During the spring of 1803, he built a boat described as "70 French feet long, 8 French feet wide, 3 French feet deep, in which he placed a Steam engine of about 8 horse power." There was "one water wheel of about 12 feet diameter on each side of the boat."[12] Each paddle wheel held ten blades.

By May 1803, the boat was finished. Smaller than anticipated, it measured only fifty-six and a half feet long (using English/American measurement) and ten and a half feet wide. It had a flat bottom, with a sharply pointed bow and stern. The boiler sat right next to the steam engine, near the center of the ship. Decking was made of heavy wood planks. To steer the steamboat, the operator controlled a rudder at the stern, using a tiller handle.

Great pride in his achievement showed in Fulton's letter to a friend in Paris, Fulner Skipwith, who had recently become a father. Fulton referred to his boat as if it, too, were a child: "My boy, who is all bones and corners just like his daddy, and whose birth has given me much uneasiness, or rather anxiety, is just learning to walk, and I hope in time he will be an active runner."[13]

Fulton invited Skipwith and his family to watch the trial run on the following Monday. "May our children," his letter concluded, "be an honour to their country and a comfort to the gray hairs of their doting parents."[14]

Bad luck had struck Robert Fulton before, and it happened again. Before the scheduled demonstration date, his steamboat sank. There was speculation that its hull might have been damaged by vandals, but no evidence of such a crime came to light.

More likely, Fulton's first boat was simply not strong enough to carry the engine's weight. So, it sank. His men worked all day and night to raise it, and then began the arduous task of rebuilding.[15] Fulton salvaged the boat's machinery, but the hull itself was beyond repair. He had no choice but to settle down for plenty of additional work.

Over the next two months, Fulton and his team constructed a new hull. By the time it was finished, the original boiler and engine were again in working condition. In July 1803, Fulton had a steamboat ready for operation on the Seine River.

The Big Day Arrives

Fulton decided to hold the steamboat's trial run in the evening on August 9, 1803. It was midsummer, so there would still be plenty of daylight, but the temperature would be more pleasant than in the hot midday sun.

Early in the day, his men put plenty of logs into the boiler, to build up all the heat and steam they could. At 6:00 P.M., Robert Fulton was ready to go. So was the steamboat.

Well-dressed gentleman and ladies lined the riverbanks to watch the unveiling. So did ordinary workers, beggars—anyone in the vicinity who might take an interest.

Would this strange creation do what was promised? Would it travel down the river under its own power? Might it blow up? Because most of the observers had seen the steam-operated factory nearby, the sounds and smells emanating from the boat's deck were familiar. But virtually no one on shore had ever seen a boat with a paddle wheel, turning lazily on its own.

Fulton had hired a crew of three, and he invited several guests aboard. Nodding in readiness, he signaled the pilot to shove off. To the amazement of the assembled throng, the small steamboat eased out onto the Seine River under its own power.

The journey began at a speed of three miles per hour. In the course of the one-and-a-half-hour demonstration, the steamboat eventually reached a velocity greater than four miles an hour.

Fulton had done it. The next day, a Paris newspaper called Fulton's trial a complete success. A French magazine described Fulton's creation as

> a boat of curious appearance, equipped with two large wheels, mounted on an axle like a chariot, while behind these wheels was a kind of large stove with a pipe, as if there were some kind of a small fire engine . . . intended to operate the wheels of the boat.

Once under way, "for an hour and a half [Fulton] produced the curious spectacle of a boat moved by wheels, like a chariot."[16]

The only thing lacking in the demonstration was speed. Despite Fulton's hope to achieve speeds as great as sixteen miles per hour, his boat managed only four miles an hour—and that was downstream, aided by the river's current.

Because a speed of at least four miles per hour was essential under the terms of his monopoly agreement in the United States, as renewed, Robert Livingston was worried.[17] Fulton responded that obtaining a more powerful steam engine would result in greater speed. In fact, Livingston's agreement with Fulton had called for a speed of eight miles per hour.

Back to England With the Submarine

Elated with his Paris success, Fulton placed an order with Boulton & Watt, in England, for a high-powered steam engine for his American steamboat. He went to England himself in 1804, partly to supervise construction of the engine.

Fulton's main reason for going, however, had nothing to do with steamboats. Instead, he wanted to pursue further his efforts on the submarine and its related weaponry. If the government of France was not interested, perhaps the political leaders in Great Britain—France's mortal enemy—would be more inclined to pay attention.

Actually, the British had already taken an interest in his work. Through an intermediary, Fulton had been invited to offer his naval-weaponry system to the British government. He left France in April 1804 and wound up staying in England for more than two years. While there, Fulton conducted experiments and tests of his submarine, torpedoes, and exploding mines.

On July 20, 1804, Fulton signed a contract with the British government, headed by Prime Minister

William Pitt, to promote "submarine bombs."[18] For his services, Fulton would be paid £200 every month, and up to £7,000 in expenses.[19] He could also receive a later bonus of £7,000 for each French ship that was destroyed by one of his explosive devices.

Early during his stay in England, Fulton drew plans for a one-man submarine called the *Messenger*. He also designed a larger ship—bigger than his *Nautilus*. Neither was built, but Fulton's attempts to sink a French ship almost succeeded.

On October 1, 1805, a ship equipped with Fulton's mines attacked French ships near the port of Boulogne. One of Fulton's mines exploded successfully, but the damage was modest and no ships were sunk. Despite that failure, the seven-hour assault, known as the Catamaran Raid, drew the attention of the public. Fulton's "intricate timing mechanism" for the mine, in particular, "was an excellent example of the inventor's skill and craftsmanship."[20]

Two weeks later, on October 15, Fulton success-fully blew up a Danish brig named the *Dorothea*. He had obtained this ship for this experimental attack, which took place while the ship was anchored. Even though this was not part of a battle, it was the first time that a large ship had been destroyed by using a mine.[21]

After the *Dorothea* test, Fulton began to exhibit some pangs of conscience. "In vessels thus attacked," he wrote, "it will be impossible to save the men—and many a worthy character must perish." This awareness caused him "some pain."[22] Some British military officers viewed such attacks as "unmanly" and "assassin-like."[23]

Five years later, Fulton took a somewhat less-worried view. He admitted that people "exclaim that it is barbarous to blow up a ship with all her crew." Although he could "lament that it should be necessary," he observed that "all wars are barbarous."[24]

Just a few months after the *Dorothea* explosion, on October 21, 1805, British Admiral Horatio Nelson defeated the French fleet at the Battle of Trafalgar. The war was over, at least temporarily. Great Britain ruled the ocean. There was no further need for Fulton's weapons of destruction. Not until the twentieth century would submarines enter the seas of battle.

Onward to America

Robert Fulton and his partner, Robert Livingston, did not get along well. They disagreed about who should pay which costs, and what percentage of the profits each man should receive. They even argued about the design of the steamboat. They distrusted each other, and Fulton feared "that Livingston would steal his ideas."[25]

Nevertheless, their partnership continued while Fulton remained in England. Livingston had the money for the American steamboat project, after all, and Fulton had the ideas.

On December 13, 1806, after spending nearly twenty years in Europe, Fulton arrived back in America. He was forty-one years old. He was ready to work on the steamboat—and to conduct further demonstrations of his submarine.

"With a sublime disregard for the fact that his torpedo project had been dismissed by two important governments, France and England," his great-granddaughter wrote long afterward, Fulton offered the rights of his "destructive machine" to the United States. He still felt that "in the hands of a righteous nation," such a device could "maintain universal peace."[26]

Fulton publicly demonstrated the power of the submarine and torpedo by blowing up a brig in New York Harbor. Naval experts observed the event on July 20, 1807. Fulton's proposal was "favorably considered" by President Thomas Jefferson.[27] In the end, though, the United States—like France and England—turned it down.

Although his concern for weaponry on the seas did not diminish, Robert Fulton turned instead to the steamboat. After all, unless a working boat went into operation soon, Livingston's monopoly might expire.

Publicity from his steamboat success in France had died down. More than three years had passed since his boat made its run down the Seine River.

Fulton moved into a boardinghouse on Broadway in New York City. He met shipbuilder Charles Brownne, who agreed to construct the hull for Fulton's American steamboat.

Robert Livingston, meanwhile, had also returned to America; but unlike Fulton, he had no need to live modestly. Instead, he returned to his family estate, Clermont, along the Hudson River in New York State.

After only half a year's work, Fulton's steamboat was ready for its first American trial. Powered by a single-cylinder steam engine, fueled by oak and pinewood, the long, slim steamboat had twin fifteen-foot paddle wheels.

On August 17, 1807, Fulton's steamboat began its first trip up the Hudson River to Albany. His boat completed the one-hundred-fifty-mile journey in thirty-three hours. Though not as swift as Fulton might have wished, it was fast enough to meet the terms of Livingston's monopoly agreement. Despite their differences, the two men were truly in business, ready to sell tickets for travel up and down the Hudson.

STEAM TRANSPORTATION IN AMERICA

Just one day after his first voyage up and down the Hudson River, Fulton was busy preparing the steamboat for regular commercial journeys. Decking was laid to conceal the boiler and mechanism.

On September 3, 1807, Fulton registered his craft as the *North River Steam Boat*. One day later, Fulton's steamboat was making regular runs up and down the Hudson. Less than a month had passed since its initial voyage.

Once in regular service, the *North River Steam Boat* departed from the Powles Hook Ferry Dock, at the foot of Cortlandt Street in New York City. In addition to space for light cargo, the boat contained three large passenger cabins.

Robert Fulton sketched the North River Steam Boat *in his notebook. Although he was not the first to invent a boat that moved by the power of a steam engine, Fulton made the idea popular in America.*

From the beginning, Robert Fulton wanted to give his passengers plenty of comfort, including luxurious meal service. "In anticipation of a good turnout of thirsty and hungry passengers" for the initial voyage, Fulton's great-granddaughter wrote later, "they laid in more brandy and rum as well as bread and butter, beef, fowls, eggs, watermelon, and sugar."[1]

Passengers were advised to have breakfast before departure. But then, promised the advertisements, "dinner will be served up exactly at 2 o'clock; tea with meats, which is also supper, at 8 in the evening; and breakfast at 9 in the morning."[2]

Long afterward, in 1856, Judge John Q. Wilson of Albany wrote an account of his steamboat voyage, when Fulton's creation first saw regular service. The trip began at six-thirty in the morning on Friday, September 4, 1807, and cost seven dollars.

"She was a queer looking craft," Wilson wrote, "and, like everything new, excited much attention, and not a little ridicule." A friend thought the trip to be foolhardy and said to Wilson: "John, will thee risk thy life in such a concern? I tell thee she is the most fearful wild fowl living, and thy father ought to restrain thee."[3]

As that 1807 trip began, spectators had filled the area. All of the boat's twelve sleeping compartments were taken. Three riders had chosen to go a shorter distance, getting off the boat before Albany. Wilson's report continued:

> All the machinery of the boat was fully exposed to view. The after part was fitted up in a rough manner for passengers; the entrance into the cabin was from the stern, in front of the steersman, who worked a tiller.
>
> Thick, black smoke issued from the chimney—steam hissed from every ill-fated valve and crevice of the engine. Fulton himself was there. His remarkably clear and sharp voice was heard above the hum of the multitude and noise of the engine. All his actions were confident and decided, unheeding the fearfulness of some and the doubts and sarcasms of others. Fulton stood erect upon the deck, his eye flashing with an unearthly brilliancy as he surveyed the crowd.[4]

Fulton's first voyage in regular service has been described as "an unqualified success."[5] Early journeys continued to draw attention from people stationed along the banks of the Hudson River, as well as those on other ships. All kinds of boats approached to get a good look at Fulton's steamboat. Passengers even signed an affidavit, affirming that the "accommodations and conveniences on board exceeded their most sanguine expectations."[6] For its initial scheduled run, the steamboat reached Albany in twenty-eight hours and forty-five minutes—more than six hours ahead of schedule.

Friends and Enemies

Operators of sailing ships along the river were not too pleased with the newfangled steamboat. Some of them even decided to sabotage the moving boat. They tried especially hard to ram its paddle wheels, jamming the mechanism.

Fulton had to protect his creation against such vandals. He had installed "paddle boxes" over the paddle wheels to prevent splashing on the decks and now he made other modifications as preventive measures to protect the steamboat from possible ramming by other vessels.

The steamboat had its share of mechanical troubles, too. Nevertheless, the vessel quickly demonstrated, without question, that steam power was workable.

During 1808 the original boat was modified substantially and called the *North River Steamboat of Clermont* (named for Livingston's home). Not until after Fulton's death would his first American steamboat become commonly known as, simply, the *Clermont*.

Fulton's team also began work on their second boat, the more luxurious *Car of Neptune*. Like the first steamboat on the Hudson River, it was constructed by Charles Brownne.

Dapper Mr. Fulton

Still unmarried at the age of forty-two, Robert Fulton was tall and handsome. Always a fashionable dresser, he customarily wore cashmere breeches, an elegant waistcoat, and silk stockings.[7] Workmen in those days dressed roughly, but Robert Fulton—still considering himself a "gentleman"—was something of a dandy.

One of his workmen described Fulton as being like "an English gentleman . . . with his rattan cane in his hand."[8] One historian noted that "his countenance bore marks of intelligence and talent. Natural refinement and long intercourse with the most polished societies both of Europe and America had given him grace and elegance of manners."[9]

"His habit was, cane in hand, to walk up and down for hours," wrote Fulton's chief engineer, Paul A. Sabbaton, many years later. "I see him now in my mind's eye, with his white, loosely-tied cravat, his waistcoat unbuttoned, his ruffles waving from side to side . . . he, all the while in deep thought, scarcely noticing anything passing him."[10]

J. B. Calhoun, who worked for Fulton in 1815, had, according to Sabbaton, "described Fulton as a tall, somewhat slender man, of fair, delicate complexion, of graceful, dignified bearing, and mild and gentle in his temper. He said: 'His workmen were always pleased to see him about his shops.'"[11]

Finally, the debonair, long-term bachelor's marital status was about to change. Not long before his first American steamboat trip, Fulton had met and fallen in love with Harriet Livingston, a cousin of his steamboat partner. A "famous beauty of the day," Harriet was described as "a handsome blond some twenty years [Fulton's] junior."[12] After announcing their engagement in August 1807, the two were married on January 7, 1808. Later that year, on October 10, their first child arrived: Robert Barlow Fulton.

Still Working on Two Fronts

Fulton filed a patent application for his steamboat on January 1, 1809. It contained more than five thousands words, as well as diagrams, tables, calculations, and a dozen illustrations.[13]

The application did not clearly demonstrate originality. Fulton "had evolved no convincing way of articulating his conviction that invention consisted of a new combination of existing elements."[14] Even so, his patent was granted on February 11, 1809.

Naval weapons were not forgotten as work on the steamboat progressed. Also in February 1809, Fulton demonstrated a "harpoon gun" for top government officials. President Thomas Jefferson and President-elect James Madison were present, but the American government chose not to purchase the device.[15]

Success at Last

By 1810, three of Fulton's boats were operating on the Hudson and Raritan rivers. Fulton's vessels had one advantage over some of the competition. His double-ended boats did not need to turn around to make the return journey. They could simply head back in the opposite direction, because the engine could supply power either way.

If a steamboat could travel so easily between points in New York State, why couldn't it steam down the Ohio River and over to the mighty Mississippi River? Why couldn't it meander all the way downriver to New Orleans, Louisiana?

In 1803, President Thomas Jefferson had acquired for the United States huge quantities of land between the Mississippi River and the Rocky Mountains, as part of the Louisiana Purchase. Meriwether Lewis and William Clark had explored the region, seeking trade routes to the Pacific Ocean. Since their return, the area had slowly begun to develop as an important center for trade.

Steamboat travel along the Hudson River soon became popular and fashionable, as depicted in this 1810 painting that shows Fulton's steamboat passing West Point.

Fulton wanted to put a steamboat on the Mississippi. He studied reports on currents, snags, and sandbars, deciding that nothing seemed to stand in the way of progress in that direction. This would not be as easy as sailing down the Hudson, which had few obstacles to navigation, but it could be done.

Because Fulton himself was busy with the fast-growing Hudson River fleet, he assigned the Mississippi River project to Nicholas Roosevelt. An experienced boatbuilder, Roosevelt worked at a shipyard in Pittsburgh, Pennsylvania, along the

Monongahela River. To power the new boat, Fulton again ordered an engine from Boulton & Watt in England.

By the autumn of 1811, the new long-distance steamboat was ready, appropriately named *New Orleans*. Piloted by Andrew Jack, the boat was to start down the Monongahela River, headed toward the Ohio River. Fifteen passengers were aboard, including Nicholas Roosevelt and his pregnant wife, Lydia.

Robert Fulton, who would not be going along, waved good-bye to the passengers as they began their journey downriver. Then, he went back to his work. As always, he was confident that his creation would perform well. He also knew this trip was necessary to try and validate the Livingston-Fulton steamboat monopoly in New Orleans Territory.

Fulton had applied for a twenty-year monopoly on the Ohio and Mississippi rivers, but it was granted only for the Territory of Orleans. Opposing such a monopoly, the Ohio legislature explained that it would "be dangerous . . . to invest a man or set of men with the sole power of cramping, controlling or directing the most considerable part of the commerce of the country for so great a period."[16] Now, Fulton's crew was setting out to prove that the monopoly they *did* get would be valid.

Fulton's crew knew they would reach a series of rapids below Louisville, Kentucky. Unharmed by the surging currents of the rapids, the *New Orleans* proceeded toward the Mississippi River, which they knew to be unpredictable. Such a journey could be slow and risky in any season, but they foresaw no particular reason to fear the weather.

Before they could even start down the Mississippi, however, nature had some noisy surprises in store for the boat's crew and passengers.

Din and Silence on the River

Ear-shattering sounds practically jolted the passengers on the *New Orleans* out of their beds. A moment earlier, many had been sleeping peacefully. Suddenly, the world seemed to be crashing and rolling all around them.

"The river itself was in constant agitation, boiling, churning, and foaming," according to a history of the earthquake. "Previously clear, it turned to a rusty brown hue and became thick." Ordinarily "bone-chilling cold," the water now became lukewarm. "In places, the river reached three times its normal speed," due to rising and falling of the water level.[17]

What could be happening? What had occurred to turn this peaceful river excursion into a nightmare, without any warning?

Observers of the scene could be excused for being frightened as "fissures opened up under the river . . . creating waves larger and more powerful than those found in oceans during storms. Water spouts shot up into the air. . . . Giant whirlpools sucked debris downward with dizzying speed."[18]

Huge logs that ordinarily lay at the river's bottom shot upward, into the air. Some boats on the river capsized, and members of their crews drowned. One long barge turned upside down, split in half. "The river was littered with smashed vessels for miles," in the vicinity of New Madrid, Missouri.[19] The mighty Mississippi River even began to flow backward—upstream—then back downstream again, "at frightening speeds."[20]

Not until later did the passengers and crews of the *New Orleans* discover that they had witnessed the first recorded American earthquake. In fact, it turned out to be the worst earthquake known to have taken place in this region—a record that still stands today.

The first shocks began just after two o'clock on Monday morning, December 16, 1811. By daylight, twenty-seven shocks had been felt. The earthquake "ripped the Mississippi valley apart, being felt as far away as the Atlantic Ocean."[21]

This massive, frightful shift of the earth's crust destroyed the town of New Madrid, situated close to the spot where the Ohio and Mississippi rivers met. In a matter of moments, the whole town had virtually disappeared. At the same time, an entire island had been swept away by the river's current.

Three days of tremors followed the original earthquake. With each new shudder of the earth,

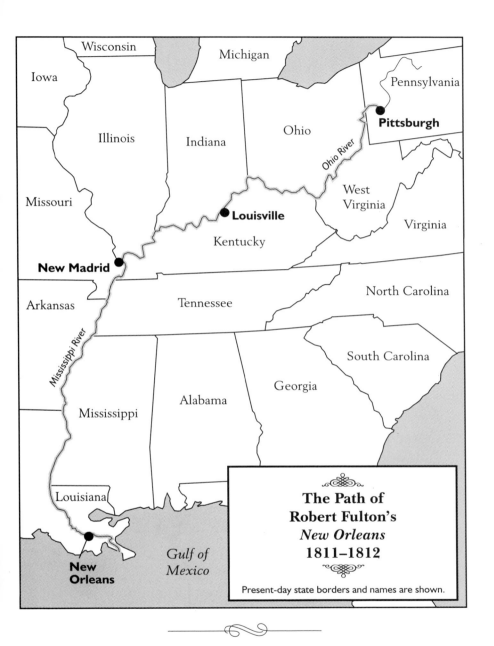

The Path of Robert Fulton's *New Orleans* 1811–1812

Present-day state borders and names are shown.

The steamboat New Orleans *left Pittsburgh, Pennsylvania, in the fall of 1811, to undertake a perilous two-thousand-mile journey down the Ohio and Mississippi rivers. In January 1812, the steamboat would arrive at New Orleans, Louisiana, after passing through a devastating earthquake at New Madrid, Missouri.*

the riders on the *New Orleans* could not be certain that another full earthquake—possibly even worse than the first one—was not about to begin.

Despite all the calamities, Fulton's boat reached the port of New Orleans on January 12, 1812. The Roosevelts' baby had been born during the arduous, 259-hour trip.

Roosevelt "was greeted by an ecstatic populace," wrote one of Fulton's biographers. "His steamboat had conquered the Mississippi."[22] On January 21 the *New Orleans* headed north to Natchez, Mississippi, with three hundred passengers and a full load of cargo. Travel farther northward, against the river current to the northern states, would have to wait until later.

Fulton's Steamboat Company Expands

Between 1807 and 1815, Robert Fulton designed thirteen steamboats. He also established an engine plant in Jersey City, New Jersey. His later boats used American engines, built from his own patents.

His creative efforts did not stop at the steamboat itself. Fulton also invented better landing slips for the docks, to make the voyages more efficient.

By 1814, fourteen paddle-wheel boats were in service on North American lakes and rivers. A revolution in transportation was beginning, fueled largely by Robert Fulton's efforts.

9

FULTON'S LEGACY

Both war and peace occupied Robert Fulton's mind in his final years. Though best known today for his passenger-carrying steamboat, eventually called the *Clermont*, Fulton continued to promote steam power for warships. He also continued to work on the submarine concept, and on ways to assault enemy vessels from beneath the seas.

In 1810, Fulton wrote a treatise called *Torpedo War and Submarine Explosion*. During the War of 1812, which was being fought by the Americans to settle problems with Great Britain that had continued after the revolution, he began to design a twin-hull, single-paddle-wheel steam battleship. Fulton hoped it would be used to defend New York

Harbor against the British blockade. Fulton, in fact, was "authorized by Congress" to construct such a ship.[1]

Named *Demologos*, the single-paddle-wheel ship would have been the first steam-powered warship. Instead of extending over the side, its paddle wheel was positioned inside the vessel, between two separate hulls. The steam engine was mounted in one hull, while boilers and stacks sat in the other. Patented by Fulton, the vessel's guns could fire a hundred-pound shell below the waterline.

Launched on October 14, 1812, the *Demologos* passed its sea trials but was never used in battle. The War of 1812 ended with an American victory before Fulton could send his ship into wartime service.

Measuring 156 feet in length, the *Demologos*—renamed *Fulton the First* later, after Fulton's death—was somewhat slow for a warship. In June 1815 it traveled fifty-three miles in eight and a half hours, averaging almost six and a half miles per hour. Even with twenty-six guns on board, the ship managed to average five and a half miles an hour.[2]

Fulton never ceased promoting steamboat travel in the West, as well as in foreign nations. In 1812 he served on a commission that recommended construction of the Erie Canal.

During the winter of 1812–1813, two men close to Robert Fulton passed away. Joel Barlow, who had served for nearly sixteen years as a friend and

"DEMOLOGOS"

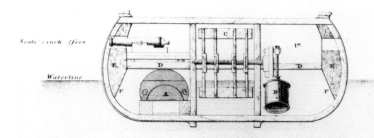

Figure 1st. Transverse section A her Boiler B the steam Engine C the water wheel
E E her wooden walls 5 feet thick, diminishing to below the waterline as at F F
draught of water 9 feet D D her gun deck

Scale ½ inch = 1 foot

Waterline

Scale ½ inch = 1 foot

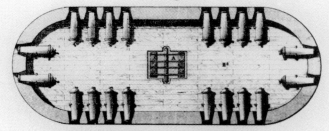

Figure 2d. This shews her gun deck 156 feet long
28 feet wide, mounting 20 guns, A the Water wheel

Figure 3d.
Side View

Scale ½ inch = 1 foot

ROBERT FULTON
November 1813

Three views of Fulton's steam warship Demologos, *drawn by Robert Fulton in November 1813.*

The launching of the steam frigate, Demologos, *later renamed* Fulton the First, *at New York on October 29, 1814.*

mentor, died in December 1812. After returning to America, Barlow had gone to Europe during the final days of Napoléon's reign. Barlow was on his way back after Napoléon's defeat at Moscow, Russia, and died in a village in Poland.

Because communication was so slow in those days, the news of Barlow's death did not reach America until late February of the following year. By then, Robert Livingston was also gone, having suffered a stroke on February 25, 1813.

Fulton was deeply affected by the deaths of his close friends.[3] He informed Edward Livingston,

Robert Livingston's younger brother, that "two such friends of such rare talents are not to be replaced in a whole life."[4]

Legal Battles Begin

Rather than fully enjoying the fruits of his success, Fulton spent some of his time attempting to fight other patents on steamboats. He also sought to suppress potential rivals who searched for loopholes in his and Livingston's steamboat monopoly. Other operators wanted a share in the growing profits that steamboats were capable of earning.

Courts continued to uphold the monopoly rights that had been granted to Robert Fulton and Robert Livingston. Not until after Fulton's death would the dispute be resolved by the United States Supreme Court.

Among the first competitors were two steamboats launched at Albany in 1811, named *Hope* and *Perseverance*. One of them, the *Hope*, even engaged in a contest against Fulton's *Clermont*, until a "collision [between them] put a stop to the race," though no serious damage was done.[5] Soon, Fulton and Livingston were granted a "perpetual injunction" against that competitor.[6]

Two other competitors presented a more serious challenge. In 1811, Aaron Ogden, a former United States senator, sought a steamboat monopoly in New Jersey. He also petitioned the New York state legislature to remove Fulton's monopoly. Ogden wanted to run his own boat, *Sea Horse*, from Elizabethtown, New Jersey, to New York City. Ogden's steamboat used a different type of engine from Fulton's, known as the "lever beam" design.[7]

In 1814, after Ogden had become governor of New Jersey, the legislature ruled in his favor. But, meanwhile, Thomas Gibbons, part owner of Ogden's boat, had opened a boat line of his own. Gibbons began to operate two steamboats adjacent to Ogden's run.

Ogden applied for, and received, an injunction against Gibbons. Even so, Gibbons continued to run the *Bellona*, defying Ogden's monopoly. Not until 1824, in a famous case known as *Gibbons* v. *Ogden*, did the United States Supreme Court finally rule against Ogden and declare all steamboat monopolies invalid.

Such a Capable Man

Steamboats are only a portion of Robert Fulton's legacy. During his lifetime, Fulton also invented a rope-making machine, a flax-spinning machine, a marble-cutting device, and a cable cutter. He developed an earth-scooping machine for canal and irrigation use. He also devised a double-inclined plane for canal navigation, even if his idea was not original.

Fulton introduced the first panorama to the French public. He invented a submarine that was capable of sending torpedoes underwater or of planting mines on enemy warships. Fulton is also credited with several improvements for canal navigation.

In addition to the *Treatise on the Improvement of Canal Navigation* and his book on torpedo warfare, Fulton's writings included an *Essay to the Friends of Mankind, Submarine Navigation,* and an essay titled *Thoughts on Free Trade.* Fulton also continued to paint, including many self-portraits, though never again as a profession.

Robert Fulton and his wife, Harriet, lived in New York City, but during the summer occupied a small house on the Livingston family estate. Not far from Clermont, their home, Teviotdale, offered an appealing view of the Hudson River—the site of what most people consider Fulton's greatest achievement. Here, he could sit in the evening and watch steamboats plying their way up and down the river.

Fulton especially enjoyed spending time with his children. In addition to their first-born son, usually called Barlow, the Fultons had three daughters—Julia, born in 1810, followed by Mary and Cornelia in the next two years.

Victim of Wintry Weather

In the winter of 1815, Robert Fulton and his lawyer, Thomas Addis Emmet, were returning from a business trip. Because no ferryboat was running, they hired a small boat to cross the Hudson River.

To reach the boat, it was necessary to walk along the ice on the frozen river. Suddenly, the ice broke, and Emmet fell into the frigid water. Fulton pulled him out of the water, but got soaked in the process. Emmet survived the mishap, but Fulton suffered from exposure.

Robert Fulton died on February 23, 1815, in New York City. He was forty-nine years old. His death brought what one biographer described as an "occasion of mourning such as was customary only in the case of the greatest public man."[8] Fulton's funeral was attended by officers of both the federal and state governments, by judges, and by "members of learned societies."[9] As part of the service, guns were fired from the *Demologos*.

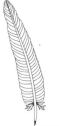

Steam in the Nineteenth Century

After Fulton's death, steam power continued to flourish for boats. For the next century and beyond, steamboats covered American rivers, carrying goods and people.

But in 1801, Richard Trevithick had built the first steam locomotive in Great Britain. By 1829 locomotives were being shipped to the United States. Two years later, Americans were building their own. The development of railroads eventually reduced the importance of canals as a means of transportation over long distances.

A year after his death, a street in New York City was renamed Fulton Street, connecting two river terminals. Nearly a century later, in 1909, the city enjoyed a centennial celebration to commemorate Fulton's achievements as well as the explorations of Henry Hudson. A procession of steamboats in Fulton's honor moved slowly down the Hudson River, led by a replica of his *North River Steamboat of Clermont.*

Left with four young children, the oldest only six, the widow Harriet Fulton moved into her parents' home. According to Fulton's will, Harriet was supposed to receive nine thousand dollars per year, with smaller amounts going to each child. But Fulton left considerably less than he had thought. In 1816 his widow married an Englishman named Charles Augustus Dale.

Looking Back: A Life of Achievement

Robert Fulton was more than an inventor, more than a businessman. He was also more than an American—closer to being a citizen of the world than one who was limited solely to his homeland.

Most men of his era led single-minded lives. From birth to death, they followed a straight-ahead path. Someone who started out as a farmer, for instance, typically remained a tiller of the soil all his life. The shopkeeper, the artisan—each tended to remain in that occupation without any deviation.

More often than not, their sons would also follow a similar, unbending path.

Not Robert Fulton. He was born in time to observe the rise of the American Revolution—right in his hometown of Lancaster, Pennsylvania. Trained as an artist during his youth in America, he spent many years in Europe, turning from art to invention. Along the way, he became acquainted with some of the leading political, cultural, and scientific figures of his day, from famed artist Benjamin West to statesman-poet Joel Barlow.

Fulton was a man of contradictions. Eventually calling himself an engineer, Fulton was also a showman and promoter. Although he claimed to be an opponent of war, he developed methods of naval warfare that some called inhumane. A businessman in later life, he could even be considered a philosopher of sorts.

By 1839, when this painting by Robert Havell was completed, steamboats traveled along the Hudson River day and night. Fulton's dream of making steamboats practical for everyday transportation had come true.

Perhaps most important, Robert Fulton helped pave the way for the new age of invention in the nineteenth century. In earlier times, great thinkers had developed their ideas mainly to demonstrate theories. Few cared whether or not their creations had any practical value. Fulton promoted a more modern approach. He insisted that to be worthwhile, any invention must have practical uses.

Two qualities helped Robert Fulton evolve into greatness. First, as a boy, and even more so as a man, he seemed utterly certain that he would succeed. Rarely did Robert Fulton exhibit any lack of confidence in his abilities. Despite a long series of setbacks and failures in his adult life, he kept on trying, and trying again. Robert Fulton never gave up.

The second key to Fulton's success was that as he evolved into an inventor, Fulton learned that it is not always essential to come up with an original idea. The person who studies the ideas of others, then transforms them into something unique and practical, can be just as important as the originator.

What Kind of Man Was Robert Fulton?

Fulton "had all the traits of a man with the gentleness of a child," wrote his chief engineer in 1857. "I never heard him use ill words to any one of those employed under him no matter how strong the provocation might be."[10]

Although it took many years, Robert Fulton achieved the fame he had sought all his life. Never a

Robert Fulton is still remembered for his many contributions to science and industry, as well as for his talents as an artist. He painted this self-portrait.

modest man, he credited himself, not others, for his achievements—even though much of his work was based on the prior efforts of his predecessors.

"American biographers have credited him with greater achievements than the facts warrant," wrote one historian. In contrast, "English writers too often have dismissed him contemptuously as a charlatan, a filcher of other men's brains, or even as a traitor."[11]

Even though few, if any, of his ideas were fully original, Robert Fulton helped usher in the age of invention. His work, therefore, helped the development of the Industrial Revolution in the United States. He helped turn the very idea of invention into a useful endeavor. A visionary man, "he saw clearly that free trade . . . between nations, universal disarmament, the spread of education and of political liberty among all people, were necessary to the progress of the human race."[12]

Americans are fortunate to have such a confident man, a persistent man, to look back on as a model for the future.

CHRONOLOGY

1765—Born on November 14 in Lancaster County, Pennsylvania, to Robert and Mary Fulton.

1773—Enters Quaker school at age eight.

1774—Father dies.

1775—American Revolution is under way.

1782—Works as artist in Philadelphia.

1786—Goes to warm springs at Bath, Virginia, to recuperate from respiratory ailment.

1787—Sails to England to study art under Benjamin West.

1791—Painting by Fulton exhibited at Royal Academy of Arts in England.

1794—Gives up painting as a profession and turns to canal navigation; British patent granted to Fulton for inclined-plane canal system.

1796—Publishes *A Treatise on the Improvement of Canal Navigation.*

1797—Goes to France to promote canal project and work on submarine; Meets Joel Barlow and wife, Ruth, in Paris; Barlow becomes close friend and advisor.

1799—Fulton's mother dies.

1800—*Nautilus* (submarine) demonstrated on Seine River in France.

1802—Establishes partnership in steamboat venture with Robert Livingston.

1803—Fulton's first steamboat operates on Seine River.

1804—Sails to England to try to sell submarine concept.

1806—Returns to the United States in December.

1807—*August*: Fulton's first American steamboat goes from New York to Albany and back.

1808—Fulton marries Harriet Livingston; Steamboat is enlarged and named *North River Steamboat of Clermont*; Second Fulton steamboat, *Car of Neptune*, is launched.

1810—Fulton writes *Torpedo War and Submarine Explosion*.

1811—Steamship *New Orleans* undertakes perilous journey from Pittsburgh, Pennsylvania, to New Orleans, Louisiana.

1812—War of 1812 begins; Fulton begins to develop warship named *Demologos*.

1815—Fulton dies in New York City.

1909—Centennial of Fulton's steamboat and Henry Hudson exploration is celebrated.

1965—Postage stamp issued in Fulton's honor.

CHAPTER NOTES

Chapter 1. Sound and Fury: Fulton's First American Steamboat

1. John S. Morgan, *Robert Fulton* (New York: Mason/Charter, 1977), p. 140.

2. Letter from Robert Fulton to Robert Livingston, quoted in Cynthia Owen Philip, *Robert Fulton: A Biography* (New York: Franklin Watts, 1985), p. 199.

3. Ibid., p. 198.

4. Ibid., p. 200.

5. Charles Todd, *Life and Letters of Joel Barlow* (New York: G. P. Putnam's Sons, 1886), pp. 233–234.

6. Morgan, p. 140.

7. Alice Crary Sutcliffe, *Robert Fulton and the* Clermont (New York: The Century Company, 1909), p. 209.

8. *The American Citizen*, August 17, 1807.

9. Quoted in Philip, p. 200.

10. Sutcliffe, p. 208.

11. Ibid.

12. Quoted in Sutcliffe, pp. 202–203.

13. Ibid., p. 203.

14. Morgan, p. 141.

15. Sutcliffe, p. 212.

16. Letter from "South Carolina gentleman," September 8, 1807, *Naval Chronicle*, 1808, vol. xix, p. 88.

17. Philip, p. 202.

18. Letter from Robert Livingston, September 21, 1807, quoted in Philip, p. 202.

19. Letter from Fulton to Robert R. Livingston, August 10, 1807, New York, quoted in Sutcliffe, pp. 197–199.

20. *The American Citizen*, August 22, 1807.

21. Philip, p. 200.

22. Sutcliffe, p. 252.

23. Philip, p. 204.

Chapter 2. One Talented Boy

1. Alice Crary Sutcliffe, *Robert Fulton and the* Clermont (New York: The Century Company, 1909), p. 23.

2. John S. Morgan, *Robert Fulton* (New York: Mason/Charter, 1977), p. 3.

3. Ibid., p. 2.

4. Sutcliffe, p. 24.

5. Ibid., p. 23.

6. Sutcliffe, pp. 21–22.

7. James T. Flexner, *Steamboats Come True: American Inventors in Action* (New York: The Viking Press, 1944), p. 112.

8. Ibid., p. 113.

9. Sutcliffe, p. 17.

10. Ibid., p. 21.

11. Cynthia Owen Philip, *Robert Fulton: A Biography* (New York: Franklin Watts, 1985), p. 7.

12. Flexner, p. 112.

13. Sutcliffe, pp. 31–32.

Chapter 3. The Budding Artist

1. Cynthia Owen Philip, *Robert Fulton: A Biography* (New York: Franklin Watts, 1985), p. 8.

2. John S. Morgan, *Robert Fulton* (New York: Mason/Charter, 1977), p. 6.

3. Alice Crary Sutcliffe, *Robert Fulton and the* Clermont (New York: The Century Company, 1909), pp. 25–26.

4. James T. Flexner, *Steamboats Come True: American Inventors in Action* (New York: The Viking Press, 1944), p. 115.

5. Ibid., p. 116.

6. Henry W. Dickinson, *Robert Fulton—Engineer and Artist—His Life and Works* (Freeport, N.Y.: Books for Libraries Press, 1913, reprinted 1971), p. 8.

7. Flexner, p. 118.

8. Ibid., p. 119.

9. Ibid.

10. Ibid.

11. Ibid., p. 117.

Chapter 4. To Europe

1. Cynthia Owen Philip, *Robert Fulton: A Biography* (New York: Franklin Watts, 1985), pp. 11–12.

2. Ibid., p. 11.

3. James T. Flexner, *Steamboats Come True: American Inventors in Action* (New York: The Viking Press, 1944), p. 119.

4. Ibid., p. 113.

5. Wallace S. Hutcheon, Jr., *Robert Fulton, Pioneer of Undersea Warfare* (Annapolis, Md.: Naval Institute Press, 1981), p. 8.

6. John S. Morgan, *Robert Fulton* (New York: Mason/Charter, 1977), p. 13.

7. Philip, pp. 12–13.

8. Ibid., p. 120.

9. Henry W. Dickinson, *Robert Fulton—Engineer and Artist—His Life and Works* (Freeport, N.Y.: Books for Libraries Press, 1913, reprinted 1971), p. 12.

10. Flexner, p. 215.

11. Ibid.

12. Dickinson, p. 12.

13. Cadwallader D. Colden, *The Life of Robert Fulton* (New York: Kirk & Mercein, 1817), p. 258.

14. Ibid.

15. Ibid.

16. Flexner, p. 216.

17. Ibid., p. 218.

18. Ibid., p. 119.

19. Ibid., p. 165.

Chapter 5. Abandoning Art for Technology

1. James T. Flexner, *Steamboats Come True: American Inventors in Action* (New York: The Viking Press, 1944), p. 220.

2. Ibid.

3. Ibid., p. 244.

4. Alice Crary Sutcliffe, *Robert Fulton and the* Clermont (New York: The Century Company, 1909), p. 49.

5. Henry W. Dickinson, *Robert Fulton—Engineer and Artist—His Life and Works* (Freeport, N.Y.: Books for Libraries Press, 1913, reprinted 1971), p. 23.

6. Flexner, p. 222.

7. Dickinson, p. 37.

8. Flexner, p. 221.

9. Ibid., p. 223.

10. John Harrison Morrison, *History of Steam Navigation* (New York: Stephen Days Press, 1958), p. 27.

11. Flexner, p. 225.

12. Wallace S. Hutcheon, Jr., *Robert Fulton, Pioneer of Undersea Warfare* (Annapolis, Md.: Naval Institute Press, 1981), p. 19.

13. Charles Todd, *Life and Letters of Joel Barlow* (New York: G. P. Putnam's Sons, 1886), p. 177.

Chapter 6. A Primitive Submarine

1. Cynthia Owen Philip, *Robert Fulton: A Biography* (New York: Franklin Watts, 1985), p. 66.

2. Ibid.

3. Ibid., pp. 72–73.

4. Wallace S. Hutcheon, Jr., *Robert Fulton, Pioneer of Undersea Warfare* (Annapolis, Md.: Naval Institute Press, 1981), p. 28.

5. Ibid., p. 29.

6. Ibid., p. 3.

7. Hutcheon, p. 18.

8. James T. Flexner, *Steamboats Come True: American Inventors in Action* (New York: The Viking Press, 1944), p. 258.

9. Quoted in Philip, p. 97.

10. Alice Crary Sutcliffe, *Robert Fulton and the* Clermont (New York: The Century Company, 1909), p. 90.

11. Ibid., p. 90.

12. Ibid., p. 93.

13. Philip, p. 113.

14. Charles Todd, *Life and Letters of Joel Barlow* (New York: G. P. Putnam's Sons, 1886), pp. 179–180.

15. Sutcliffe, p. 94.

16. Ibid., p. 95.

17. Todd, pp. 180–181.

18. Hutcheon, p. 49.

19. John S. Morgan, *Robert Fulton* (New York: Mason/Charter, 1977), p. 67.

20. Ibid., p. 122.

Chapter 7. Fulton's First Steamboats

1. James T. Flexner, *Steamboats Come True: American Inventors in Action* (New York: The Viking Press, 1944), p. 277.

2. Alice Crary Sutcliffe, *Robert Fulton and the* Clermont (New York: The Century Company, 1909), p. 118.

3. Cynthia Owen Philip, *Robert Fulton: A Biography* (New York: Franklin Watts, 1985), p. 121.

4. John S. Morgan, *Robert Fulton* (New York: Mason/Charter, 1977), p. 118.

5. Charles Todd, *Life and Letters of Joel Barlow* (New York: G. P. Putnam's Sons, 1886), p. 198.

6. Ibid.

7. Sutcliffe, p. 34.

8. Flexner, p. 280.

9. Sutcliffe, p. 139.

10. Flexner, p. 282.

11. Sutcliffe, p. 124.

12. Quoted in Sutcliffe, pp. 123–124.

13. Ibid., p. 148.

14. Ibid.

15. Flexner, p. 291.

16. Sutcliffe, p. 149.

17. Morgan, p. 132.

18. Wallace S. Hutcheon, Jr., *Robert Fulton, Pioneer of Undersea Warfare* (Annapolis, Md.: Naval Institute Press, 1981), p. 72.

19. Ibid., pp. 67, 72.

20. Ibid., p. 78.

21. Ibid., p. 86.

22. Letter from Fulton to "Mamy" West, October 16, 1805, quoted in Hutcheon, p. 87.

23. Hutcheon, p. 88.

24. United States Congress, *American State Papers, Naval Affairs*, vol. 1, p. 223.

25. Flexner, p. 283.

26. Sutcliffe, pp. 174–175.

27. Ibid.

Chapter 8. Steam Transportation in America

1. Cynthia Owen Philip, *Robert Fulton: A Biography* (New York: Franklin Watts, 1985), p. 204.

2. Advertisement for *North River Steamboat*, in Alice Crary Sutcliffe, *Robert Fulton and the* Clermont (New York: The Century Company, 1909), insert.

3. Account of *Clermont* voyage by Judge John Q. Wilson, quoted in Sutcliffe, pp. 246–249.

4. Ibid.

5. Ibid., p. 205.

6. Sutcliffe, p. 251.

7. Philip, p. 180.

8. James T. Flexner, *Steamboats Come True: American Inventors in Action* (New York: The Viking Press, 1944), p. 317.

9. James Renwick, *Life of Robert Fulton* (New York: Harper, 1845), p. 203.

10. Paul A. Sabbaton, Fulton's chief engineer, letter to J. F. Riegart in 1857, quoted in Sutcliffe, p. 217.

11. Description by J. B. Calhoun, quoted in Sutcliffe, p. 217.

12. Morgan, p. 150.

13. Philip, p. 233.

14. Ibid.

15. Ibid., p. 237.

16. Quoted in Philip, pp. 280–281.

17. William Atkinson, *The Next New Madrid Earthquake* (Carbondale: Southern Illinois University Press, 1989), p. 12.

18. Ibid., p. 12.

19. Ibid., p. 13.

20. Ibid.

21. Ibid., p. 1.

22. Philip, p. 275.

Chapter 9. Fulton's Legacy

1. Alice Crary Sutcliffe, *Robert Fulton and the* Clermont (New York: The Century Company, 1909), p. 175.

2. Henry W. Dickinson, *Robert Fulton—Engineer and Artist—His Life and Works* (Freeport, N.Y.: Books for Libraries Press, 1913, reprinted 1971), p. 264.

3. Cynthia Owen Philip, *Robert Fulton: A Biography* (New York: Franklin Watts, 1985), p. 290.

4. Letter from Robert Fulton to Edward Livingston, March 29, 1813, quoted in Philip, p. 290.

5. Dickinson, p. 244.

6. John Harrison Morrison, *History of Steam Navigation* (New York: Stephen Days Press, 1958), p. 39.

7. Ibid.

8. Dickinson, p. 266.

9. Ibid.

10. Paul A. Sabbaton, Fulton's chief engineer, letter to J. F. Riegart in 1857, quoted in Sutcliffe, p. 217.

11. Dickinson, p. vii.

12. Ibid., p. 267.

GLOSSARY

aqueduct—Structure that permits water in a canal to flow over a river in its path.

berth—Bed or bunk that serves as sleeping quarters in a boat.

bow—Front end of a boat.

breeches—Short trousers for men, fitting snugly at the knee.

burgess—A political representative in local government of colonial America.

catamaran—Boat with two hulls, side by side.

coffeehouse—A meeting place and lodging house, where rooms are rented.

cravat—Fancy scarf, worn as a necktie.

injunction—Court order requiring that someone refrain from engaging in a specified act.

loophole—Provision in a law that permits a person to engage in an action that evades the intent of that law.

mine—Explosive device that can be attached to an enemy ship's hull.

monopoly—Right granted by a court to conduct business without competition from other companies.

periscope—Device that allows a person in a submarine to see above the surface of the water.

provincial—Lacking the sophistication of urban life.

rattan—Tough stem of a type of palm tree, used to make walking sticks (canes).

sloop—Type of sailing ship, with a single mast and sails at both fore and aft.

socialism—Political doctrine that stresses cooperation rather than competition.

stern—Rear end of a boat.

submarine—Boat that is capable of submerging below the surface of water and moving, equipped with breathing apparatus for occupants.

switch—Short, flexible whip.

tanning—Process of transforming animal skin into leather.

torpedo—Explosive projectile that can be shot from one boat to an enemy ship, traveling beneath the surface until it explodes.

Tory—Supporter of the British government against the colonial independence movement.

utopian—People who believed in an ideal state, stressing harmony and cooperative effort. Utopians believed communities could be developed in which people lived in total harmony and peace.

waistcoat—Ornamental vest, worn under an outer coat by men in colonial America.

FURTHER READING

Books

Bowen, Andy Russell. *A Head Full of Notions*. Minneapolis: Carolrhoda Books, 1997.

Flexner, James T. *Steamboats Come True: American Inventors in Action*. New York: The Viking Press, 1944.

Hutcheon, Wallace S., Jr. *Robert Fulton, Pioneer of Undersea Warfare*. Annapolis, Md.: Naval Institute Press, 1981.

McCormick, Anita Louise. *The Industrial Revolution in American History*. Springfield, N.J.: Enslow Publishers, Inc., 1998.

Morgan, John S. *Robert Fulton*. New York: Mason/Charter, 1977.

Philip, Cynthia Owen. *Robert Fulton: A Biography*. New York: Franklin Watts, 1985.

Internet Addresses

H.W. Dickinson. *Robert Fulton: Engineer and Artist*. December 1996. <http://www.history.rochester.edu/steam/dickinson> (February 3, 1999).

Library of Congress. *American Treasures of the Library of Congress: Reason*. March 23, 1997. <http://lcweb.loc.gov/exhibits/treasures/trroz4.html> (February 3, 1999).

Robert H. Thurston. *"Makers of America": Robert Fulton: His Life and its Results*. December 1996. <http://www.history.rochester.edu/steam/thurston/fulton> (February 3, 1999).

INDEX